# THE MEASU1

# The Measures of Medicine

## Benefits, Harms, and Costs

Richard K. Riegelman, MD, PhD

Blackwell
Science

**BLACKWELL SCIENCE**
**Editorial offices:**
238 Main Street, Cambridge, Massachusetts 02142, USA
Osney Mead, Oxford OX2 0EL, England
25 John Street, London WC1N 2BL, England
23 Ainslie Place, Edinburgh EH3 6AJ, Scotland
54 University Street, Carlton, Victoria 3053, Australia
Arnette Blackwell SA, 1 rue de Lille, 75007 Paris, France
Blackwell Wissenschafts-Verlag GmbH, Kurfürstendamm 57, 10707 Berlin,
Germany
Blackwell MZV, Feldgasse 13, A-1238 Vienna, Austria

**Distributors:**

*North America*
Blackwell Science, Inc.
238 Main Street
Cambridge, Massachusetts 02142
(Telephone orders: 800-215-1000 or
  617-876-7000)

*Australia*
Blackwell Science Pty Ltd
54 University Street
Carlton, Victoria 3053
(Telephone orders: 03-347-5552)

*Outside North America and Australia*
Blackwell Science, Ltd.
c/o Marston Book Services, Ltd.
P.O. Box 87
Oxford OX2 0DT
England
(Telephone orders: 44-865-791155)

Acquisitions: James Krosschell
Development: Coleen Traynor
Production: Lee Medoff
Manufacturing: Kathleen Grimes
Typeset by Huron Valley Graphics, Ann Arbor, MI
Printed and bound by Braun-Brumfield, Ann Arbor, MI

© 1995 by Blackwell Science, Inc.
Printed in the United States of America
95 96 97 98 5 4 3 2 1

**Library of Congress Cataloging in Publication Data**

Riegelman, Richard K.
    The measures of medicine : benefits, harms, and costs / Richard K.
Riegelman.
        p.     cm.
    Includes bibliographical references and index.
    ISBN 0-88542-280-X
    1. Medicine—Decision making—Data processing.   I. Title.
    [DNLM: 1. Decision Support Techniques. 2. Cost-Benefit Analysis.
W 74 R554m   1995]
R859.7.D42R53   1995
362.1—dc20
DNLM/DLC
for Library of Congress                                        94-37064
                                                                    CIP

# CONTENTS

# PREFACE

## A Guide to the Guidelines

Decision trees, sensitivity analyses, discount rates . . . the tools of quantitative decision-making intimidate and mesmerize. Yet one cannot pick up a health journal without seeing a decision tree, a cost effectiveness equation, or a guideline based on these tools of quantitative decision-making.

Students and practitioners of medicine and public health can be deterred by jargon. We may only read and memorize the recommendations, rather than reading between the lines and examine the foundations of official recommendations. This book is designed to take both the mystery and the magic out of quantitative decision-making.

Quantitative decision-making is inherently complex because it requires us to spell out everything. It makes us examine every possible outcome, estimate every relevant probability, reveal our most personal values, and perhaps most important confront how much we do not know. The very complexity of quantitative decision-making can be viewed as a virtue if it allows a better understanding of ourselves and our decision-making process.

Once you get beyond the initial aura of complexity the principles of quantitative decision-making can provide an important framework for structuring your thinking about how decisions are made. In addition, quantitative decision-making helps us to see and understand the basis for differences of opinion.

Quantitative decision-making is a relatively new approach that had to fight to win its place at the decision-making table. Perhaps to convince the unconvinced of its importance, its advocates have often called it "rational" decision-making. In *The Measures of Medicine* it is called quantitative decision-making or decision-making by the numbers, so that it is not viewed as the one and only right way to make decisions.

*The Measures of Medicine* was written for students and practitioners of both clinical medicine and public health. These two professions have for too long represented mutually exclusive perspectives for viewing health issues. Clinicians looked through the eyes of the individual patients, whereas those in public health viewed the world from a population perspective taking into account the impact on the entire community or society. The structure of quantitative decision-making lets us see the connections between these perspectives as well as the reasons different conclusions are reached.

Part I focuses on benefits and harms and how they form the basis for individual decision-making. The expectation that benefits will exceed harms is a prerequisite for selecting a treatment in quantitative decision-making. Increasingly, however, it is not the end of the issue: costs cannot be ignored. It is possible to consider costs as one of the harms, or, alternatively, to regard a benefit that exceeds the harms as only a recommendation to treat if the individual or society can afford the treatment. The latter approach will be used in *The Measures of Medicine*.

At the social or community level, costs are central to the decision-making process. Thus, Part II focuses on the issues of costs and incorporates them into the process of decision-making along with benefits and harms.

*The Measures of Medicine* walks readers through the process of quantitative decision-making one step at a time, stressing the assumptions which are being made each step of the way. The text of the book is designed to cover the key issues necessary for critical reading of the quantitative decision-making literature. Footnotes and suggested readings are provided for those who want to know more about the subtleties and controversies that remain.

The appendix is designed to summarize the steps and assumptions, thereby providing an overview of the process. It can be a useful reference as one begins to read the literature. The accompanying *Computer Exercises in Medical Decision Making* is designed to help you practice the principles contained in the text. It also aims to help you learn a bit about your own decision-making style and risk-taking attitudes.

The first and hardest step in the decision-making process is the decision to begin. *The Measures of Medicine* is designed to make that first step a little bit easier.

# ACKNOWLEDGMENTS

The writing and rewriting of *The Measures of Medicine* took place over a four year period—from 1990 through the summer of 1994. Developing and testing the approach and making sure it was consistent with the evolving concepts of decision analysis and cost-effective analysis was a challenge that required the assistance of a large number of my students and colleagues.

I am indebted to Mary Ann Baily Ph.D., a health economist who read and reread the cost-effectiveness chapters making sure I stayed within the accepted concepts of cost-effectiveness. Among those who read drafts of chapters and provided invaluable advice are Robert Hirsch Ph.D., W. Scott Schroth M.D., M.P.H., Robert Jayes M.D., Jackie Glover Ph.D., Daniel Rubenson Ph.D., and Shoshanna Sofaer Dr.P.H. In addition, Cathy Tucker provided important assistance, especially with all those decision trees.

Much of the writing of *The Measures of Medicine* was done during my sabbatical at the University of Chile. Drs. Matilde Maddeleno and Ramon Florenzano provided me with the opportunity to write and to try my emerging ideas out on a stimulating group of residents and faculty.

The staff of Blackwell, under the direction of James Krosschell, have once again demonstrated their commitment to producing quality publications and their willingness to experiment with ways to produce educational materials.

Students in the M.D. and the M.P.H. programs at The George Washington University Medical Center provided a critical testing ground to make sure the material really worked. Their comments and encouragement helped polish the final version.

As always, my wife Linda has played an indispensable role in my writing, tolerating my distractions and letting me know when my writing works and when it still needs another revision.

# INTRODUCTION

## Decision-Making by the Rules and by the Numbers

*The Measures of Medicine* transports us to the community of Simplicity at the turn of the twenty-first century to see what can be learned about the process of quantitative decision-making or decision-making by the numbers.

We are about to enter a very different world. In our experiences with decision-making in health care, we generally have relied on rules rather than numbers. In Simplicity, in contrast, we will rely on the numbers. Thus, we need to distinguish between two different approaches: qualitative decision-making using rules and quantitative decision-making using numbers.

Decision-making by the rules starts with two basic goals. One basic goal is to produce benefit. By benefit we mean an improvement in the health outcome of those who receive the treatment. The rules for achieving benefit are then expressed in more familiar terms, such as treatments of choice or indications for treatment.

In addition to the goal of achieving benefit there is a second goal of avoiding harm. By harm we mean a reduction in the quality of health. This goal is often incorporated in the expression, *first do no harm*. In medicine, rules are usually derived from this principle and are expressed as contraindications.

In practice, the goals of producing benefit and avoiding harm often come into conflict with each other and require that we choose between them. In medicine, this choice is usually made by defining relative contraindications to treatment. In rule based decision-making, however, the rule maker is careful not to trade-off one goal for another. There can be exceptions to the rule, but the rules are still the rules.

Decision-making by the numbers is based on the same fundamental goals, but it aims to achieve these goals in a very different way. Decision-making by the numbers starts with the premise that all decisions are trade-offs, balancing the chances of benefits against the chances of harm.

Quantitative decision-making starts with probabilities that are used to express the chances of benefits and also the chances of harms. These probabilities are then adjusted to take into account the quality of health resulting from each potential benefit and harm. Decision-making using numbers is then performed by selecting the option in which the benefits exceed the harms to the greatest extent.

Thus, decision-making by the rules and by the numbers both aim to produce benefit and avoid harm. Rule-based decision-making asserts, however, that these goals are best achieved by defining rules and then deciding which rule best applies in a particular situation. Decision-making by the numbers asserts that the best choice is the one in which measurement of the potential benefits exceeds the measurement of potential harms to the greatest extent.

Part I looks at the process of decision-making by the numbers by exploring how we can measure the benefits and the harms. We will start by examining how the measures of benefits and the measures of harms can be used to make recommendations for taking care of patients; we also explore the recommendations produced by these numbers.

Part II looks at how the process of quantitative decision making can be used to make recommendations for entire communities or societies. To accomplish this process, we need to incorporate more numbers in the form of financial costs. By incorporating costs, we come face to face with the often painful choices confronted by the citizens of Simplicity as they deal with the measures of medicine: benefits, harms, and costs.

Enough philosophy, it is time to begin our journey to the community of Simplicity.

# PART

# I

## Benefits and Harms

# CHAPTER ONE

## Probabilities

The January 15, 1999 issue of The Old England Journal of Medicine reported the first cases of what came to be called the Sudden Adult Disability Syndrome (SADS). The initial cases all occurred among residents at University and Big City Hospital in a community called Simplicity. You have applied for residency training at University Hospital and Big City Hospital.

SADS was reported as occurring among previously healthy residents. The initial cases all became acutely ill in their on-call rooms without any evidence of trauma, drugs, or foul play; they all died within weeks. The only early symptoms experienced by all these residents was that on the day before they became ill they each told a colleague that they were "feeling old."

During 1998 there were 20 cases of SADS among the 200 residents at Big City Hospital. There were also 20 cases of SADS among the 500 residents at University Hospital. As a physician about to begin your residency training during the new century you are more than a bit concerned about your chances of acquiring SADS. Thus you ask yourself:

AT WHICH HOSPITAL IS THE CHANCE OF DEVELOPING
SADS GREATEST?

From what we know let us see what we can say about the chances of developing SADS at University and Big City Hospital.

In order to compare University and Big City Hospitals we need to have a standard method for measuring and comparing our chances. Probabilities are our basic measuring instrument for making the comparisons that are the basis for medical decisions. Let us start by looking at what probabilities are and why we need them.

Probabilities measure how many times something occurs compared to how many times it could have occurred. It may not be obvious why it is necessary to compare probabilities. Why not just count the number of times an event occurs in two situations such as SADS at University Hospital and Big City Hospital?

If the number of cases of SADS is used as the only basis for comparison, the hospital with the largest number of residents is always at a disadvantage in any comparison. If we compare only the number of cases of SADS at Big City and University Hospitals, the two hospitals look the same; 20 cases of SADS at each during 1998.

Looking at what happened compared with or relative to what could have happened is the only fair comparison. As a potential resident in one of these hospitals, you should be interested in more than the number of times SADS occurred. You should be concerned about the number of times it occurred relative to the number of times it could have occurred among residents at each hospital. Thus comparing probabilities will give you a better idea of the chances of developing SADS for any one particular resident.

Now how do we calculate the probability of SADS at University Hospital and Big City Hospital? The probability of developing SADS at University Hospital in the one year time period of 1998 is a fraction with the following numerator and denominator:

$$\frac{\text{Number of times the event occurred}}{\text{Number of times it could occur}}$$

or, in other words

$$\frac{\text{Number of times the event occurred}}{\text{Number of times it occurred} + \text{number of times it did not occur}}$$

The number of occurrences of an event is known as the *frequency* of an event. The number of times an event could occur is known as the *number of observations*. Thus probabilities can be measured as:

$$\frac{\text{Frequency of the event}}{\text{Number of observations}}$$

The frequency or the number of events that occurred during a year of residency is measured by counting the number of residents in whom SADS developed during the year. The observations are the number of residents who are each observed during the same year of residency.[1]

Thus the probabilities of SADS in the two hospitals are:

$$\text{Big City Hospital} = \frac{20 \text{ cases of SADS in 1998}}{200 \text{ residents}}$$

$$= \frac{.1 \text{ case of SADS}}{\text{resident}}$$

$$\text{University Hospital} = \frac{20 \text{ cases of SADS in 1998}}{500 \text{ residents}}$$

$$= \frac{.04 \text{ cases of SADS}}{\text{resident}}$$

Thus the probability of developing SADS among residents at Big City Hospital was .1 while the probability of developing SADS among residents at University Hospital was .04.

Probabilities can have numerical values from 0 to 1. A probability of 1 implies that an event occurred on every observation. A probability of 0 implies that an event did not occur on any observation. Thus, probabilities are always fractions. For any one observation, an event either occurs or it does not occur. When using probabilities for making decisions we often speak of the chances of an event occurring rather than the probability. When we refer to chances, we often use percentages.

Fortunately probabilities can be converted into percentages by merely multiplying the probability by 100%. Thus, a probability of .1 is equivalent to 10% and a probability of .04 is

---

[1] Because one observation represents one resident observed for one year the units used to measure observations are often called *person-years*, or in our scenario resident-years. When there is a unit of time in the denominator the resulting measurement is known as a *rate*.

equivalent to 4%. Thus, we often interchange probabilities and percentages.

Probabilities or percentages provide us with the basic scale of measurement used in decision-making. We use probabilities or percentages to measure the chance of occurrence of benefits as well as the chance of occurrence of harms. Probabilities or percentages then allow us to measure and compare the chance of benefit compared to the chance of harm.

Before we attempt to compare the probability of developing SADS in Big City and University Hospitals we need to be sure that all cases of SADS are identified so that the numerators are equally complete. We also need to be sure that an observation in the denominator has the same meaning in both hospitals. That is, an observation implies one resident training in the hospital that is being studied for one year. Thus, in this situation it is important that we do not call each resident's entire residency training one period of observation because not all residents train for the same number of years.

From what we know so far, it would be hard to miss a resident with SADS. In addition, we have defined an observation the same way in both hospitals: one year of training by one resident. Therefore, we can use the probabilities we have obtained to compare the chances of developing SADS in University and Big City Hospitals.

Whenever we want to compare situations and make a decision between two or more options, such as accepting a residency at University or Big City Hospital, we can use what is called a *decision tree*. The use of decision trees to assist us in making choices is often called *decision analysis*.

A decision tree is a widely used graphic technique that attempts to display the choices being considered and the consequences of each of these choices. To accomplish this goal, a decision tree starts with a square called a *choice node* or decision node. A choice node is represented as a square, with alternative choices branching from the square. The choice or decision node indicates that the decision-maker can select one of the two or more alternative actions.

Decision trees require us to structure decisions so that we must choose one alternative from among two or more choices. The choices available to us in a decision tree are displayed on the

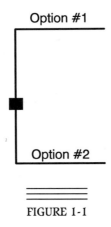

FIGURE 1-1

horizontal lines which connect with the choice node. Thus the decision tree starts as displayed in Figure 1-1.

It is possible to display additional alternatives as demonstrated in Figure 1-2

In *The Measures of Medicine,* our choices will be limited to 2 or 3 alternatives. Regardless of the number of choices, a description of each treatment option or alternative will be placed along the horizontal lines that connects to the choice node.

In addition to choice nodes that are displayed as squares, decision trees contain *chance nodes* that are displayed as circles. Chance nodes, as opposed to choice nodes, imply that what immediately follows is not under our control. Once a choice is made between treatment options, it is usually followed by more than one possible outcome. Decision analysis assumes that each outcome occurs with a known probability.[2]

Figure 1-3 displays the decision tree for our choice between University Hospital and Big City Hospital. The square choice node is the place to start. Extending up from the choice node is a vertical line which connects to the horizontal line with the label University Hospital; that is one alternative. Extending down and

---

[2] The particular circumstances of a patient or skill of a clinician may influence these probabilities. However, when using decision trees for individual patients these special circumstances are assumed to be known prior to making the decision and included in the probabilities used in the decision tree.

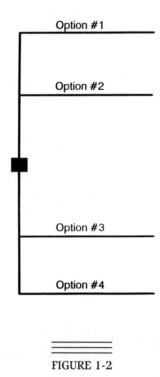

FIGURE 1-2

then horizontal from the choice node is the second alternative: Big City Hospital. At the end of these horizontal lines we reach a chance node indicated with a circle.[3]

The reason for constructing decision trees is to help us make decisions. Therefore, examine Figure 1-3 and make the following decision:

**DO YOU PREFER TO BE A RESIDENT AT UNIVERSITY OR BIG CITY HOSPITAL?**

Did you choose University Hospital because the decision tree displays a lower probability of developing SADS. That is a per-

---

[3] Choice nodes may occur two or more times within a decision tree. This is frequently the situation when we want to represent a treatment option which requires several steps. In *The Measures of Medicine*, there will only be one choice node located at the left-hand side of the decision tree.

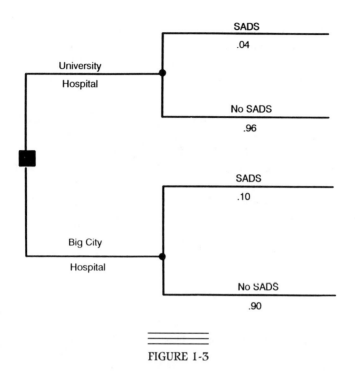

FIGURE 1-3

fectly reasonable conclusion to reach based on the decision tree. However, you need to recognize that you have taken at least three things for granted. You have made a series of assumptions.

1. You have assumed that University and Big City Hospital were your only choices. That is, you have assumed that the decision tree accurately reflects your options.
2. You have assumed that the probabilities in the decision tree were accurately estimated and included all the important probabilities that influence your decision. For instance you may be assuming that everything else of importance to you is equal in the two hospitals. In addition you are assuming that your probability of developing SADS would be the same as the average of all residents.
3. You have assumed that the probabilities derived from a past period accurately reflect the probabilities in the future. In an epidemic, the number of susceptible individuals way decline over time, thus reducing the overall probability of develop-

ing the disease. Alternatively the presence of those with the disease may increase the probability of new cases in the future. Thus, past probabilities may not always be good predictors of future probabilities. [4]

Now we have examined how we calculate probabilities, the basic measurement tool used in quantitative decision making. We have seen how we can include probabilities in decision trees and thus compare the probabilities of potential outcomes of two of more different choices such as the choice to be a resident at University or Big City Hospital. Now let us take a look at how we can use probabilities and decision trees to examine the results of an intervention that can result in more than two potential outcomes.

━━The epidemic of SADS produced a furious search for potential therapies. In recent years a new drug called FOREVER has been successful in the prevention of rapid aging. Thus there was considerable interest in studying the effects of FOREVER on residents.

In July, 1999, 400 residents at University Hospital agreed to participate in the study. Half the residents were randomized to receive FOREVER and half were randomized to receive a placebo. The results of the one year study were as follows:

FOREVER GROUP: Four of the 200 residents developed and died from SADS. In addition 2 residents developed a side effect of FOREVER known as "youthful indiscretion." Youthful indiscretion produced immediate death.

PLACEBO GROUP: Eight of the 200 residents developed and died from SADS.

[4] In *The Measures of Medicine* we also assume that the outcome states occur only once. However, in many disease states outcomes may be temporary and/or may occur repeatedly. More complicated models of these process using what are called *transition probabilities* can be used. When two or more disease states occur in succession, transition probabilities can be incorporated into decision analysis using what are called *Markov processes*.

> It is now July 2000 and you are a busy resident at Univer-
> sity Hospital. You have little time to think about the chances of
> developing SADS. However one of the first decisions you
> need to make as a resident at University Hospital is:        ■

## WILL YOU TAKE FOREVER AS A RESIDENT AT
## UNIVERSITY HOSPITAL?

We can use the results of the previous study to obtain the probabilities we need to construct a decision tree if we are willing to
assume that the results of the 1999 study will accurately predict
what will happen to your group of residents. In the FOREVER
group 4 of the 200 residents developed SADS. Thus the probability of developing SADS after taking FOREVER at University
Hospital was

$$\frac{4}{200} = \frac{2}{100} = .02$$

Similarly we can calculate the probability of side effects of
FOREVER as follows. There were 2 residents who developed
the side effect thus the probability of the side effect is

$$\frac{2}{200} = \frac{1}{100} = .01$$

For the other treatment option, the alternative to take no
treatment, we can use the probability of developing SADS obtained from the placebo group in the study. In the placebo group
there were 8 residents among the 200 who developed SADS,
thus the probability of developing SADS was

$$\frac{8}{200} = \frac{4}{100} = .04$$

Figure 1-4 displays the result of the treatment option to use
FOREVER compared to the alternative of no treatment (No
Rx). Again notice that the available treatment options follow the
choice node and precede the chance node. The possible outcomes
are then displayed after the chance node. For the option to use
FOREVER the three possible outcomes are SADS, side effects,

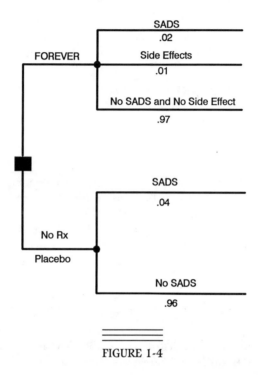

FIGURE 1-4

and no SADS and no side effects. For no treatment the two possible outcomes are SADS and no SADS.

The number under each of the possible outcomes is the probability of occurrence of that outcome. The only probability which we have not yet obtained is the probability of no SADS and no side effects. However, we can obtain this probability from what we already know. We can obtain the probability of No SADS and no side effect if we are willing to assume that these three outcomes are the only three possible outcomes. Since everyone must have one of the outcomes, the probability of the three possible outcomes must add up to 1 or 100%. Thus we can calculate the probability of No SADS and no side effects by adding together the other probabilities and subtracting their sum from 1.

Probability of no SADS and no side effects =
1 − [(probability of SADS) + (probability of side effects)]

=1 − (02 + .01) = .97

Similarly for the no treatment alternative the probability of no SADS is equal to:

$$1 - \text{probability of SAD} =$$
$$1 - .04 = .96$$

Figure 1-4 displays the option to use FOREVER and also the option of no treatment (No Rx). Remember that this decision tree is constructed using the previous data from University Hospital.

The probability of the three outcomes of FOREVER add up to 1 or 100%. In order for this to occur we have made the assumption that SADS and also the side effect cannot both develop in the same individual. This is known as the *mutually exclusive* assumption.[5]

How can we express the results of this decision tree? One way is to look directly at the difference in probabilities between the outcomes of treatment when FOREVER is taken and when no active treatment is taken. Here the outcomes of developing SADS and developing the side effect of FOREVER are the same, i.e., death. Thus, we can express the difference in the probability of death as:

Probability of death with no active treatment − probability of death with FOREVER =
$$.04 - (.02 + .01) = .04 - .03 = .01$$

A difference in probabilities of .01 may have meaning for you but for many people decimals are hard to interpret. This difficulty becomes increasingly true as our decision trees get more complicated. An alternative way to express the results of a decision analysis is known as a *number-needed-to-treat*. The number-needed-to-treat is calculated by dividing one by the difference in probabilities, or in mathematical language, by taking the reciprocal. Thus the number-needed-to-treat is:

$$\frac{1}{.01} = 100$$

[5] The *mutually exclusive* assumption makes little difference as long as the probability of developing SADS and the probability of developing the side effect are both small. However, when these probabilities are large, there can be a substantial probability of experiencing both events. The probability of experiencing both events by chance, if one event does not alter the probability of experiencing another event, is the product of the two or more probabilities. Thus, if the probabilities of two events are .01 and .02 then the probability of experiencing both events is $(.01)(.02) = .0002$ or .02%. However, if the probabilities of experiencing two events are .20 and .30 then the probability of experiencing both events is $(.20)(.30) = .06$ or 6%.

The number-needed-to-treat is a useful number to help us summarize what is gained by our decision to use FOREVER. It tells us that, on average, for every 100 residents who take FOREVER there will be one less case of SADS. Therefore, the number-needed-to-treat tells us how many residents, on average, need to be treated with FOREVER to reduce by one the number of cases of SADS.

In general, a positive number-needed-to-treat indicates the number of individuals who need to be treated, on the average, to produce one less harm such as death or to produce one more benefit such as cure. Using probabilities directly it may be difficult to determine whether the difference in probabilities between the options is substantial or clinically important. It is often easier to address this important question using the number-needed-to-treat.

Now we have explored how we can use probabilities to decide between options in which there are more than two potential outcomes. We have seen that the results of a decision analysis can be expressed as differences in probabilities or as a summary measurement known as the number-needed-to-treat. It is important to recognize however, that the difference in probability and the number-needed-to-treat are calculated based on the data in one particular setting. When extending or extrapolating the decision to other settings we need to be very careful, as illustrated in the next decision.

---

■■You decide to take FOREVER during your first year of residency at University Hospital. During the second year residents are often assigned to train at Community Hospital where the chance of developing SADS during a year of training has been 1.6%. ■■

---

WOULD YOU TAKE FOREVER AS A RESIDENT AT COMMUNITY HOSPITAL WHERE THERE IS A 1.6 % CHANCE OF DEVELOPING AND DYING FROM SADS?

Figure 1-5 displays the alternatives at Community Hospital. Community Hospital differs from University Hospital in an important way. At Community Hospital the probability of de-

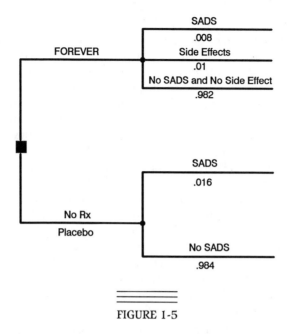

FIGURE 1-5

veloping SADS in the absence of preventive treatment is .016 compared to .04 at University Hospital. The lower probability of developing SADS at Community Hospital means that we cannot expect the benefits of using FOREVER to be as impressive as at Community Hospital.

At University Hospital FOREVER reduces the probability of developing SADS from .04 to .02. In other words FOREVER reduces in half the probability of developing SADS. Now if we assume that FOREVER has the same effectiveness at Community Hospital, we would also expect it to reduce by half the probability of SADS. At Community Hospital this reduction by half would reduce the probability from .016 to .008. Notice that even though we are still reducing the probability by half, the size of the reduction is only .016 to .008, (i.e., a difference of .008) compared to a reduction from .04 to .02 (i.e., a difference of .02) at University Hospital. Thus, in Figure 1-5 the probability of SADS if FOREVER is chosen is .008 and the probability of SADS if the no treatment alternative is chosen is .016.

Taking FOREVER at Community Hospital may also produce the side effect of FOREVER, i.e., youthful indiscretion. At University Hospital the probability of developing the side effect was .01 among those who took FOREVER. Unless there is reason to believe otherwise we assume that the probability of developing the side effects will be the same for those who choose FOREVER at Community Hospital as it was at University Hospital. Therefore, in Figure 1-5, the probability of side effects is .01.

Thus, it is more difficult to produce a *net benefit* at Community Hospital. By net benefit we mean the benefit minus the harm. This is the case because of the lower chance of developing SADS at Community Hospital even with the no therapy alternative. When using FOREVER at Community Hospital it is just as likely to produce a harm as when used at University Hospital. In other words, at Community Hospital compared to University Hospital for those who choose to take FOREVER there is a lower probability of benefit but the same probability of harm. Thus the net benefit is less at Community Hospital.[6]

Now take a look at Figure 1-5. Remember that everyone who develops SADS dies. Thus, when using FOREVER at Community Hospital the probability of deaths with FOREVER and with no treatment are as follows:

$$\text{FOREVER} = \frac{\text{Probability of death from SADS + probability}}{\text{of death from side effects}}$$

$$= .008 + .01 = .018$$

No treatment = probability of death from SADS

$$= .016$$

Now we can calculate the difference in probabilities of death between no treatment and taking FOREVER at Community Hospital:

$$\left(\begin{array}{c}\text{Probability of death with}\\\text{no active treatment}\end{array}\right) - \left(\begin{array}{c}\text{Probability of}\\\text{death with FOREVER}\end{array}\right)$$

$$= .016 - .018 = -.002$$

[6] For benefit we assume that the probability of developing SADS is reduced by the same proportion. In University and Community Hospital we are assuming that in each hospital the probability of developing SADS will be cut in half. Thus for benefits we assume an equal proportion benefit. A proportion is a special type of ratio or fraction in which the numerator is a subset of the denominator. For harms we make another assumption. We assume that the difference in probability of developing side effects between the FOREVER group and the Placebo group will be the same in each hospital. Thus, for harms we assume that at each hospital side effects will occur in 1% or with .01 probability. Thus we are assuming that the difference between the harms due to treatment and no treatment is the same at the two hospitals.

What does this difference in probability tell us? To get a better feeling for the results let us take the reciprocal and calculate the number-needed-to-treat:

$$\frac{1}{-.002} = -500.$$

A number-needed-to-treat of $-500$ implies that, on average, for every 500 individuals who are treated with FOREVER one more will experience the adverse outcome, (i.e., death), compared with those undergoing no treatment. A positive number-needed-to-treat indicates the number of individuals, on average, who need to be treated to produce one more desirable outcome. A negative number-needed-to-treat indicates the number of individuals, on average, who need to be treated to produce one more unfavorable outcome.

There is an important principle about treatment decisions which are illustrated by the decision trees from University Hospital and Community Hospital. The results tell us that in one setting, the benefits of a therapy may be greater than the harms, whereas in a second setting, the same therapy may have harms which are greater than the benefits.

Now let us see how we can use probabilities and decision trees to decide whether to use more than one treatment.

---

■The epidemic of SADS produced a large number of new therapies. It was soon recognized that with good supportive care 10% of patients made a spontaneous and complete recovery from fully developed SADS. This occurs whether or not FOREVER has been taken previously. Effective treatment, however, was clearly needed.

In response to the SADS epidemic the world wide medical computer system, known as KNOW-IT-ALL, set to work searching its files for possible molecular structures to test on residents once they developed SADS. A new drug known as AGELESS was identified and tested.

Because FOREVER had already been shown to have effectiveness in the prevention of SADS at high risk hospitals such as University Hospital with a probability of developing SADS of .04, the investigators studied AGELESS in addition to FOREVER. First they tested whether AGELESS should be used for those who developed SADS despite having taken FOREVER.

The study randomized residents at all high risk hospitals in Simplicity to two groups. One group was prescribed FOR-EVER and received AGELESS if they developed SADS. This group was called FOREVER-then-AGELESS. The second group was prescribed FOREVER and received placebo if they developed SADS. This group was called FOREVER. In both groups the probability of developing SADS after taking FOR-EVER was .02 while the probability of side effects from FOR-EVER was .01. A total of 100 residents in each group developed SADS. The results once SADS developed were as follows:

FOREVER-then-AGELESS: Fifty residents recovered, five developed and died as a result of side effects of AGELESS, and 45 died of SADS.

FOREVER: All residents developed complications of SADS, 90 residents died from the complications of SADS, and 10 recovered completely.     ▬

## AT UNIVERSITY HOSPITAL WHERE SADS IS STILL OCCURRING WITH A PROBABILITY OF .04 SHOULD AGELESS BE USED IF SADS DEVELOPS AFTER TAKING FOREVER?

Let us see if we can construct a decision tree displaying the option FOREVER-then-AGELESS and alternatively the option FOREVER.

To begin let us focus on FOREVER. Remember that previously everyone who developed SADS died. Now there is a 10% chance of complete recovery from SADS or a probability of .1 of recovery. Thus we need to add a new chance node after the development of SADS. At this chance node there is a .1 probability of complete recovery and a .9 probability of dying from SADS.

The bottom half of Figure 1-6 displays FOREVER. It incorporates the probability of .1 of complete recovery after SADS develops. Notice that we now have two chance nodes, one following the other. This implies that there is now no decision to be made whether to treat SADS if it develops. Everyone who develops SADS will be treated with supportive treatment. However, there is a chance that the outcome will be recovery, and a chance it will be death. Also notice that the two chance nodes follow each other from left to right implying that the development of SADS occurs earlier in time before the outcome of death or recovery.

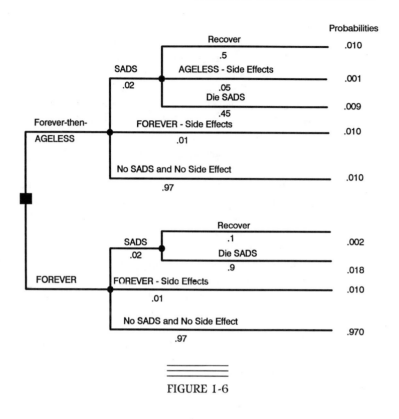

FIGURE 1-6

Now let us see how to construct a decision tree for the option to use FOREVER-then-AGELESS. This decision tree is exactly the same as the option to take FOREVER alone except for the treatment and subsequent outcome after SADS develops. With the use of FOREVER at University Hospital where SADS still occurs with a probability of .04, use of FOREVER reduces the probability of developing SADS to .02.

When AGELESS is used after FOREVER we need to add a chance node followed by different probabilities and different outcomes. Once SADS develops, recovery now carries a .5 probability, since 50 of the 100 with SADS recovered. Side effects of AGELESS have a .05 probability, since 5 of the 100 residents with SADS developed and died of side effects. The probability of dying from SADS is .45, since 45 of 100 residents with SADS died.

This decision tree is more complicated; it includes more data than we can easily retain and manipulate in our heads. To help organize increasingly complicated decision trees, we will now start to place the overall probabilities of each of the final outcomes at the right-hand side of the decision tree. One of the greatest advantages of decision trees is that they allow us to draw out the possibilities and see all the data in one place. They allow us to be sure we have considered all the potential options and all the potential outcomes.[7]

Once the decision tree has been constructed and all the probabilities have been inserted further steps are necessary to summarize the decision tree. When we looked at decision trees using FOREVER this process was very straightforward. We looked directly at the probabilities of death in the FOREVER group and in the no treatment group and compared the results.

The current comparison requires that we take two additional steps. These steps are often called *folding back* and *averaging out*. Folding back implies that for each potential outcome of each of the options (i.e., recover, die from SADS, or die from side effects) we need to calculate its probability of occurrence by multiplying more than one probability.

These probabilities are calculated as follows. Let us start at the upper right of the decision tree in Figure 1-6 and identify the first potential outcome of one of the options. This is the outcome recover after developing SADS with the FOREVER-then-AGELESS option. The probability of recovering after developing SADS with FOREVER-then-AGELESS is calculated by multiplying the probability of recovering after developing SADS (.5) times the probability of developing SADS after taking FOREVER (.02). Thus, the probability of ending up on this particular branch of the decision tree is calculated by multiplying together (.5)(.02) = .01. Because we have begun at the right side of the decision tree and moved to the left or backward this process is called *folding back* the decision tree.

In the process of folding back, we followed along a path and

---

[7] In real decisions there are often far more possible outcomes than displayed in our decision trees. When drawing decision trees for real problems it is often helpful to initially include all the potential options and all the potential outcomes. Then, you can eliminate those options that do not seem viable and can eliminate those branches of the remaining options that are extremely unlikely to occur or are of only slight importance if they do occur. This process is known as *pruning back* the decision tree.

calculated the probability of obtaining one particular outcome. The probability we obtain for any one particular outcome is called a *path probability*. In our example, the path probability of recovery after developing SADS is .01. This path probability appears as the right upper probability of the decision tree in Figure 1-6.

The same path probability would have been obtained if we had moved from left to right following the natural course of events. That is, we could have multiplied (.02)(.5) instead of (.5)(.02) and still obtained the same results. The path probabilities appear one under the other at the right end of the corresponding branches of the decision tree.

When this process of multiplying probabilities is performed another important assumption is made. We are assuming that the occurrence of one event, such as the development of SADS in the group receiving only FOREVER, does not influence the occurrence of the subsequent event, such as the probability of recovery after developing SADS. This is known as the *independence* assumption.

It is often natural to make the independence assumption even when we don't realize that we are making an assumption. We make the independence assumption, for instance, when we calculate the probability of obtaining two heads on two flips of a coin. If the coin is flipped fairly, each flip has a .5 probability of coming up heads. The result on the first flip does not influence or affect the results on the second flip. This lack of influence of one flip on the next is what we mean by independence. Notice that independence does not mean that both events cannot occur. Rather, it implies that the probability of more than one event occurring is assumed to be obtained by calculating the multiplication product of the probabilities of two or more events.

The independence assumption is so important in decision making that it deserves some special attention. At times you may not agree with the independence assumption. For instance we may suspect that after taking FOREVER the probability of recovery after developing SADS is more (or less) likely to occur compared with the probabilities of recovery if FOREVER is not taken. We might suspect that FOREVER continues to have a protective effect and increases the chances of recovery if good supportive care is provided. Alternatively, we may suspect that prior use of FOREVER weakens the body's own natural defense mechanisms and actually reduces the probability of recovery if SADS actually develops.

Thus, we may suspect based on what we know from research or what we believe based on our clinical experience that the events included in a decision tree are not independent at least for a particular patient. If so, it is possible to alter the probabilities in the decision tree to reflect this lack of independence. However, reliable information to determine if the independence assumption actually holds true is not often available. Thus, we often need to merely assume it is true and at least initially act as if it were true. As with all our assumptions, however, it is important to understand what is being assumed so we can better recognize those situations where the assumption is violated or does not reflect what is actually occurring.

Now that the decision tree has been folded back and the path probabilities of each potential outcome has been calculated, we are ready to summarize the decision tree using a process called *averaging out*. Averaging out a decision tree involves adding the potential outcomes of a particular option. In this case we add the probability of each outcome which results in survival.

Thus, for the FOREVER-then-AGELESS option the probability of survival is .98; that is .97 (no SADS–no side effect) plus .01 (recovery from SADS). With FOREVER, the probability of survival is .972, that is .97 (no SADS and no side effect) plus .002 (recover from SADS).[8]

To get a better idea of what these two probabilities .98 and .972 imply, the number-needed-to-treat can be calculated as follows:

$$\frac{1}{\text{(probability of a desirable outcome with FOREVER-then-AGELESS)} - \text{(probability of a desirable outcome with FOREVER alone)}}$$

$$\frac{1}{.98 - .972} = \frac{1}{.008} = 125$$

Thus, the number-needed-to-treat indicates that, on average, 125 individuals need to be treated with the FOREVER-then-AGELESS approach to produce one more survivor compared

---

[8] In making these calculations we assumed that survival produces the same quality of health whether it occurs because SADS does not develop or because of recovery from SADS. Likewise, we assume that death is death whether it occurs because of SADS or because of the side effect of one of the drugs. We will discuss how we measure quality of health in Chapter 2.

with use of the FOREVER alternative. The number-needed-to-treat does not directly indicate whether the FOREVER-then-AGELESS approach should be used but it does provide an understandable measurement of what we can expect to happen if the probabilities are accurate.

What is meant by probabilities being accurate? The meaning is different when we are applying the results to groups of individuals versus when we are interested in applying the results to one particular individual (i.e., a patient). When we are considering applying the same treatment to a group of similar individuals we are interested in the percentage of the patients who will experience a particular outcome.

However, when we are dealing with potential outcomes for one particular patient, the patient will only experience one of the potential outcomes. Probabilities or percentage then refer to the chances that each of the outcomes will occur for that particular patient. Most patients are not the average patient, for any one potential outcome they have a higher chance or a lower chance than the average patient. Thus, when dealing with individual patients it is natural for us to try to individualize the probabilities using what are called *subjective probabilities*.

Individualized probabilities require additional information about factors that predict outcomes. These *prognostic factors* can help select an individual's treatment. For SADS, however, we do not have information on prognostic factors. Therefore we are acting as if each resident has the same probability of responding to treatment i.e., the average probability.

Probabilities estimated by clinicians for individual patients using objective or subjective prognostic factors may be more accurate than using probabilities that reflect the average patient. However, if these prognostic factors can be measured they can be used to better estimate the probabilities that are actually included in a decision analysis.[9]

---

[9] Clinical experience often forms the basis for subjective probabilities. This may include knowledge of the previous morbidity or mortality data for physicians or for institutions. These subjective probabilities may be developed by clinicians even when data is not available. Clinical experience can be less accurate than objective data for estimating probabilities. Clinical experience may be inaccurate for several reasons including: small numbers, selective follow-up, and selective recall of events. In addition treatments which produce dramatic and immediate results such as surgery may be viewed as having a greater probability of success than treatments which are longer term and less clearly connected to the outcomes such as nutritional interventions.

Now we have examined the method we can use to construct decision trees when treatments are combined. In order to perform the calculations we need to make important assumptions, such as the mutually exclusive assumption and the independence assumption. To the extent that these and other assumptions are not fulfilled in the particular clinical situation we are examining, our numbers and thus our results will not be accurate. Nonetheless, we often need to make assumptions and proceed to make decisions.

When we looked at one treatment at a time we recognized that benefits and harms do not act in the same way when we extrapolate then to new settings. Benefits and harms also do not act in the same way when we combine treatments as we will now see.

---

■The prognosis of SADS after complications occur was so poor that clinicians decided to define a condition known as SADS with complications. It was decided to recommend both FOREVER and AGELESS whenever SADS with complications was diagnosed. A new combined pill was marketed as FOREVER-plus-AGELESS.

New studies from the laboratory demonstrated that SADS affected newly discovered secret of youth cells (SOY cells). In addition it was recognized that FOREVER had a different effect on SOY cells than AGELESS. Thus, it was possible to separately determine whether each of these treatments had its desired effect on SOY cells after being administered. Therefore, by examining the effect on SOY cells it was now possible to determine whether FOREVER was successful and separately determine whether AGELESS was successful even when they were both administered together.

Studies of patients who developed SADS with complications demonstrated that both FOREVER and AGELESS needed to be successful in reversing the damage to SOY cells for the treatment to cure those with SADS with complications. Thus, success with one treatment alone did not produce cure. Studies also demonstrated that when these treatments were used after SADS with complications had occurred the probability of fatal side effects was much higher.

Studies showed the following chances of success and side

effects when the combined treatment was used on those patients with SADS who developed complications.
>   FOREVER is successful 50% of the time
>   AGELESS is successful 20% of the time

Immediately fatal side effects occur from both FOREVER and
from AGELESS.
>   FOREVER side effect now occurs 6% of the time
>   AGELESS side effect now occurs 4% of the time
>   In comparison Standard Treatment continued to result in
complete recovery with a probability of .1 and death with a
probability of .9.                                        ▬

## SHOULD THE COMBINATION FOREVER-plus-AGELESS BE RECOMMENDED FOR PATIENTS WHO DEVELOP SADS WITH COMPLICATIONS?

Before looking at the decision tree that displays this decision,
think about and decide whether you prefer to use the FOREVER-
plus-AGELESS combination or Standard Treatment which results in 10% survival.

Figure 1-7 displays the choice between using both FOR-
EVER-plus-AGELESS and the other option which is to use
standard supportive care (Standard Treatment). Are there other
options? No, we are acting as if these are the only viable options. Now notice that this decision tree starts from a different
point than our other decision trees. It starts with everyone already having SADS. Other decision trees started at a point in
time before SADS had developed.

Decision trees can begin at any point we wish before or
after the disease develops, before or after diagnosis, before or
after complications develop. However, if we wish to directly
compare one option to another in terms of its probabilities or
number-needed-to-treat, then each option must begin at the
same point in the course of the disease. Thus all options in a
decision tree can begin before a disease develops, before complications, or after complications—but we cannot mix starting
points.

Because we are beginning at the point where individuals already have developed SADS, our decision tree potentially applies

to all individuals who develop SADS. This decision tree is potentially applicable to individuals at University Hospital, Community Hospital, Big City Hospital or wherever else SADS develops. This is the case, because despite the different probabilities of developing SADS, we have no reason to believe there are different probabilities of dying or recovery from SADS once it develops.

Now look at the outcomes of the two options we are considering. With the Standard Treatment the probability of recovery is .1 and the probability of death is .9. With the combination pill FOREVER-plus-AGELESS things are more complicated. First it is not obvious how to construct the decision tree for the combination pill. Decision trees attempt to reflect the course of events with later events coming to the right of earlier events in the decision tree. However, in our scenario, two treatments or events occur simultaneously. We therefore need to decide which drug to display as occurring first. Fortunately, it

FIGURE 1-7

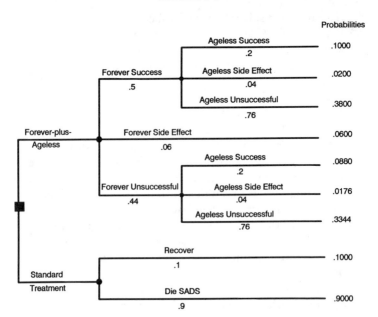

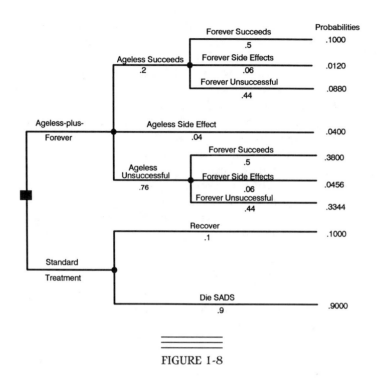

FIGURE 1-8

does not matter. The overall results will be the same either way. Figure 1-8 displays the combination treatment as if AGELESS was given first.[10]

We can calculate the path probabilities for each of the specific outcomes by making the independence assumption and multiplying the probabilities which lead to a specific outcome. For instance the probability that FOREVER will be successful and that AGELESS will also be successful is $(.2)(.5) = .1$. Each of these path probabilities is displayed on the right hand side of the decision trees in Figures 1-7 and 1-8.

---

[10] The specific outcome mix, however, will be somewhat different. For instance 4% of individuals will die of side effects of AGELESS if we draw a decision tree as if AGELESS is given first. If we draw the decision tree as if FOREVER is given first then 1.76% of individuals will die of the side effects of AGELESS. When the outcomes of different treatments cannot all be regarded as live or die then the order of treatment can make a difference.

The method used to combine or average out these path probabilities depends on what events are necessary to produce survival and what events will result in death. From what we know about the use of FOREVER-plus-AGELESS once SADS with complications occurs, it is necessary for both treatments to be successful for the individual to survive. If one treatment is successful and the other is unsuccessful death still occurs. Thus, the only path probability which results in survival is the FOREVER successful and the AGELESS successful path probability that we have already calculated to be .1 or 10%. This is exactly the same probability of survival that occurs with Standard Treatment in the bottom of Figures 1-7 and 1-8.

The probability of survival (and thus the probability of death) are the same if we use the FOREVER-plus-AGELESS combination pill or alternatively if we use only Standard Treatment. Why has this result occurred?

Look again at the data. Remember

FOREVER is successful 50% of the time
AGELESS is successful 20% of the time

Immediately fatal side effects occur from both FOREVER and from AGELESS.

FOREVER side effect occurs 6% of the time
AGELESS side effect occurs 4% of the time

To determine the probability of occurrence of an outcome we need to decide whether the outcome is an **and** outcome or whether it is an **or** outcome. **And** outcomes require that both events occur before the outcome will occur. **Or** outcomes require that either of the events occur before the outcome occurs. An approximation of the probability of **and** outcomes can be obtained by multiplying the probability of the two events. Thus, if success with FOREVER *and* with AGELESS is necessary for cure to result we need to multiply the probability of success with FOREVER times the probability of success with AGELESS.

An approximation of the probability of **or** outcomes can be calculated by adding the probabilities of the two events. Side effects here are an example of an **or** outcome. They can occur at any step in the process. Thus the probability of side effect is approximated by adding the probability of side effects from FOREVER to the probability of side effects from AGELESS.[11]

If probabilities of success are multiplied, a probability of $(.5)(.2) = .1$ is obtained. If the probabilities of harm or side effects are added, a probability of $(.06) + (.04) = .1$ is obtained. Often it is necessary for two or more successful events to occur before the benefit of treatment occurs. In contrast, harms can occur at any step along the way. Thus, calculation of the probability of benefits often requires multiplication while calculation of the probability of harms often requires addition.

When we multiply probabilities to obtain a probability of both events occurring, we obtain what is called an *intersection* or *conjunction of probabilities*. When we add probabilities to obtain a probability of one or the other of the events occurring we obtain what is called a *union* or *disjunction of probabilities*.

When deciding whether to use the combination of FOR-EVER-plus-AGELESS, did you expect the combination to be better than Standard Treatment? If you did you engaged in a common practice: overestimating the probability of benefits and underestimating the probability of harms. The tendency to overestimate benefits and underestimate harms is a natural consequence of the fact that the probabilities of success of FOR-EVER and of AGELESS (i.e., .5 and .2) are so much larger than the probabilities of side effects (i.e., .06 and .04).

Now we have seen that we need to be very careful in drawing conclusions about harms and benefits especially when we extrapolate harms and benefits to a new setting or when we automatically combine two treatments such as FOREVER and AGELESS. However there are other ways to combine treatment. Sometimes we will offer a second treatment only after the failure of a first treatment. Let us take a look at how we can analyze the results of this type of combination of treatments.

---

■Clinicians were of course frustrated when they began to appreciate that FOREVER-plus-AGELESS was no better in a combination pill than Standard Treatment for SADS with complications.

---

[11] These calculations are approximations because they make the independence assumption and the mutually exclusive assumption.

First they tried treating SADS with complications by lowering
the dosages of both treatments hoping that they could continue
the successes while lowering the side effects. Unfortunately
successes were reduced but most side effects remained.

Then they thought there might be a better way to use
FOREVER and AGELESS as separate treatments if they could
begin treatment at the first sign of SADS rather than waiting
for complications. By testing SOY cells it was possible to
define a condition which became known as early SADS as
distinguished from SADS and from SADS with complications. Fortunately, it is now possible to recognize early SADS
by its effect on SOY cells. Perhaps by monitoring the SOY
cells and looking for success or failure of the first treatment the
one treatment alone might be adequate for some patients.
Then the other treatment could be held in reserve for those
patients who failed the first treatment. Thus, some patients
treated at the first sign of SOY cell problems might be successfully treated even though they receive only one treatment.

To their great satisfaction this approach worked well. The
probabilities of complete recovery using FOREVER alone and
also using AGELESS alone in early SADS were exactly the
same as the previous probabilities of success for each treatment
alone. That is for early SADS FOREVER alone resulted in a
50% chance of cure and AGELESS alone resulted in a 20%
chance of cure. The probabilities of side effect also remained
the same at 6% for FOREVER and 4% for AGELESS. Thus,
this new approach looked promising. For treatment of early
SADS one full strength treatment was clearly better than the
combination of FOREVER-plus-AGELESS. However, now
you are faced with another decision.                      ▬

### SHOULD FOREVER OR AGELESS BE GIVEN FIRST IN TREATMENT OF EARLY SADS?

Figure 1-9 displays the outcomes resulting from the option to
give FOREVER first and use AGELESS only if FOREVER fails
as well as the option to give AGELESS first and use FOREVER
only if AGELESS fails. The decision tree indicates each of the
path probabilities. Notice here that as opposed to treatment of
SADS with complications, use of either AGELESS or FOR-

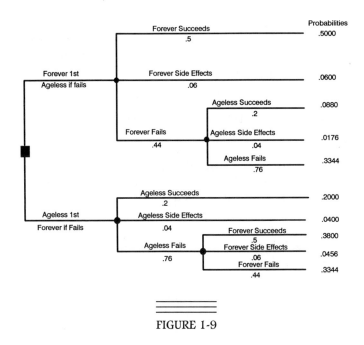

FIGURE 1-9

EVER carries a probability of preventing the development of SADS. Thus, there is more than one way of preventing SADS; either AGELESS can succeed or FOREVER can succeed.

To obtain the overall probability of preventing SADS, we average out the decision tree. We need to add together the probability of preventing SADS through success of FOREVER to the probability of preventing SADS through the success of AGELESS.

Looking at Figure 1-9 we can calculate these probabilities. Figure 1-9 displays the two treatment options FOREVER-first-AGELESS-if-fails and the option to use AGELESS first.

In order to summarize the decision tree we take the following steps:

1. First we obtain the path probability of each outcome. We do this by multiplying the probabilities of each of the events that occur along a particular path. When there is only one event along a path this probability in and of itself is the path

probability. Thus, the path probability in the FOREVER-first-AGELESS-if-fails option is .5000 for FOREVER succeeds. When there is more than one event and thus more than one probability along a path the probabilities are multiplied to obtain the path probability. Thus, with FOREVER fails (probability = .44) followed by AGELESS succeeds (probability = .2) the path probability is (.44)(.2) = .0880. All the path probabilities are presented on the right hand margin of the decision tree.

2. The path probabilities which result in cure are added. There is more than one path which results in cure. Cure can occur if FOREVER succeeds or if AGELESS succeeds. Thus we can add the path probabilities FOREVER succeeds plus the path probability AGELESS succeeds. In the FOREVER-first-AGELESS-if-fails option we add together the probabilities .5000 plus .0880 and obtain a probability of cure of .5880.

Using the AGELESS-first-FOREVER-if-fails option we obtain cure with a probability of .2000 from AGELESS initially, and .3800 when FOREVER is used after AGELESS fails. Thus, the probability of cure is .2000 plus .3800 or .58 (i.e., 58%). Both of these options are far better than using Standard Treatment with its 10% chance of cure.

We will now call these options FOREVER-first and AGELESS-first. The results for FOREVER-first and AGELESS-first are very similar to each other. To understand how they compare to each other we can calculate the number-needed-to-treat using FOREVER-first compared with using AGELESS-first as follows:

$$\frac{1}{.588 - .580} = \frac{1}{.008} = 125$$

This number-needed-to-treat indicates that, if these probabilities are accurate, the FOREVER-first option will produce, on average, one additional survivor every 125 times it is used compared with the AGELESS-first option. Everything else being equal this is a worthwhile advantage favoring FOREVER-first.

The treatment options we have just examined produce expected outcome that are quite close. When we are faced with this type of close call we often need to examine how sensitive the results are to the numbers we have used in the decision tree. In order to examine whether a choice of alternatives might be affected by the numbers we include, we can perform what is known as a *sensitivity analysis*. Let us look at one form of sensitivity analysis.

---

■■The researchers at University Hospital thought they could improve upon this therapy for early SADS by using a new technique for administering AGELESS. At University Hospital they found that with a new commercially available device called EXTEND the fatal side effects of AGELESS can be reduced from 4% to 2.6%.                                              ■■

---

## USING EXTEND, SHOULD AGELESS BE USED BEFORE FOREVER?

Figure 1-10 incorporates Extend into both treatment options and displays the options to use FOREVER-first and alternatively to use AGELESS-first. Compare Figure 1-9 which displays the same options without using EXTEND to Figure 1-10 which incorporates EXTEND. The side effects of AGELESS are now .026 instead of .04. Those who do not develop the side effect when EXTEND is used are assumed to move into the AGELESS (with EXTEND) succeeds category. AGELESS' side effect falls from .04 to .026 or by .014. AGELESS (with EXTEND) succeeds increases by the same .014. Therefore in Figure 1-10 AGELESS (with EXTEND) succeeds has a probability of 0.214.

The next step is multiplying the probabilities along each path of the decision tree, that is fold back the decision tree. These path probabilities for each potential outcome are indicated at the right hand side of the decision tree. Finally, average out by adding the outcomes which results in cure. In the FOREVER-first option we add together the outcome in which FOREVER succeeds (probability of .5000) to the outcome in which AGELESS (with EXTEND) succeeds (probability of .094) to obtain a probability of cure of .594.

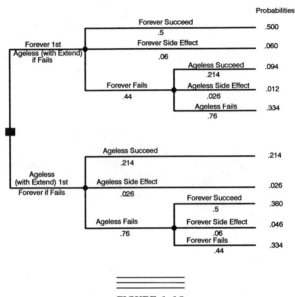

FIGURE 1-10

AGELESS-first and FOREVER-first now have exactly the same probability of resulting in cure or survival. Both approaches have a .594 probability of survival. The probability of survival with both approaches has increased by using EXTEND. However, the probability of survival with AGELESS (with EXTEND) first has increased more. When the probability of the outcome of interest is equal when using either of two different options the results are called a *toss-up*. The numbers that produce a toss-up can give us some useful information for our decision-making.

By again folding back and averaging out the decision trees, some important information has been gained. The probability of fatal side effects of AGELESS needs to be considerably smaller than .04 before it makes sense to use it first. If the probability of a fatal side effect of AGELESS is less than .026, it makes sense on the basis of the information we have incorporated into our decision tree to use AGELESS-first. If the probability of a fatal side effect of AGELESS is greater than .026, it is better to use FOREVER-first.

This probability of fatal side effects of AGELESS (.026) is called a threshold or *threshold value*. A threshold value indicates that the decision is a toss-up, i.e., the outcomes produced by the two choices are the same. The search for thresholds is part of a process in decision analysis known as *sensitivity analysis*. It is a process of determining how sensitive our decision is to the numbers we use.

Decision trees can help structure our options and help us see how sensitive our choice of options is to changes or differences in the probability of benefits or harms. This process can help us determine if small improvements are enough to make us change our recommended choice between options. It can also be very helpful when data or experts disagree on the probabilities. In both situations we can fold back or recalculate the path probabilities and then average out the decision tree again to see if the results are different.

A modest advance in therapy may or may not be enough to make a difference in the choice between options. Two experts may disagree about a probability but their disagreement may or may not make a difference in which option the decision tree recommends. Thus, decision trees can be useful in determining whether a difference or a disagreement about probabilities makes a difference in which option produces the best results.

After much research two forms of treatment for SADS have now become acceptable alternatives. FOREVER-first and AGELESS-first have each provided us with treatments for early SADS in which the benefit exceeds the harm. However, as we will soon see, they have not stopped the epidemic of SADS.

So far we have examined the use of decision trees to evaluate the probabilities of adverse outcomes such as death. We have seen how we can compare treatments; how we can extrapolate from one setting to another; how we can combine therapies in several different ways; and how we can test whether the recommendations are sensitive to the probabilities which we include in the decision analysis.

However, up until now we have acted as if there are only two potential outcomes: cure and death. In addition we have acted as if these outcomes can occur only in the immediate future. Now let us turn our attention to how we can deal with situations with more than just cure or death as potential outcomes. Then we will examine a situation when a potential outcome does not occur in the immediate future.

# CHAPTER TWO

# Utilities and Timing

## UTILITIES

The SADS epidemic continued to spread with more and more cases presenting every year among individuals who had never worked in a hospital or been hospitalized. The probability of developing SADS each year in Simplicity is now 1 per 1,000 or .001. Without good preventive measures for the general population, clinicians are left with treating early SADS with FOREVER-first. Alternatively based on personal preference or professional judgement AGELESS-first is used.

One morning in early 2004 as you begin your medical practice, you receive an urgent message from the World Institute for Science and Health (WISH). As you turn on your computer you read about the newest advance in the world-wide battle against SADS.

WISH has just approved a new treatment for those who develop SADS. It is called RESTRICT. This agent is a powerful new treatment for SADS that can be used instead of FOREVER-first or AGELESS-first. RESTRICT is able to save the life of 90% of those in whom early SADS develops.

These 90% make a complete recovery with one important exception. Unfortunately RESTRICT has an important side effect—it causes destruction of voluntary muscle in everyone who survives. WISH informs you that RESTRICT has initially been approved for use in practice for early SADS only for those who refuse to take FOREVER or AGELESS. The decision whether to recommend RESTRICT should be based on "clinical judgement." ▄

## WILL YOU RECOMMEND RESTRICT TO YOUR PATIENTS WITH SADS?

Some simplifications have been necessary to allow us to summarize the results of our decision trees for treatments of SADS. We needed to act as if there were only two possible outcomes of treatment: death and full recovery or cure. Death could occur as the result of a side effect of FOREVER, a side effect of AGELESS, or SADS. Similarly, recovery could occur after taking FOREVER, after taking AGELESS, or after developing SADS.

When summarizing the decision trees these probabilities of death and cure are added. This approach clearly involves a simplification of reality: a useful simplification, however, because it allowed us to avoid the difficult question of measuring different qualities of health. Now, however, we cannot avoid this issue any longer.

The outcome after taking RESTRICT is clearly different than full recovery and it is different than death; its worth is somewhere in between. Thus, we need to look at more than the probability of harms and benefits; we need to examine the quality of health resulting from the harms and benefits.

A concept known as *utility* is used to measure the relative preferences for different outcomes. Utilities imply that a particular outcome has different worth or value to different individuals. Utilities, as opposed to probabilities, are inherently perceived or subjective measures of quality of health; they reflect the relative importance that an individual places on a particular outcome. Utilities aim to measure the intensity or strength of an individual's preferences.

The utility of varying degrees or different types of disability differs from person to person. A choice of dialysis versus kidney transplantation, medical versus surgical management of coronary artery disease, or chemotherapy versus observation for metastatic cancer may tilt one way or the other depending on doctors' and patients' utilities for different outcomes. Our goal is to develop a scale that allows scoring of utilities. The scoring results in a numerical value measured on the same measuring scale that was used to measure probability. By using the same measuring scale we can combine utilities and probabilities.

First we need to review the characteristics of the scale we use for measuring probabilities. The measuring scale for probability has the follow features; (1) The scale extends from zero to one and there are no negative numerical values. (2) There is an unlimited number of equally spaced categories between 0 and 1. To collect data on utility, it is necessary to provide the same scale. Thus, the limits of the utility scale are set at 0 and 1.

The upper end of the scale, 1, is usually defined as the individual's state of full health. Sometimes when dealing with medical decisions 1 is equated to cure. The exact definition of 1 may vary and can influence the results. Cure of a patient's current problem may not put them back at what they would regard as 1, or their full health. The lower end of the scale is more precise; it represents death. Although, this end state is easier to visualize, it assumes that there is only one way to get there. We made the assumption that death was death no matter how one gets there. We also acted as if recovery is the same regardless of how one gets there.

The following scale is our measuring system for measuring utilities. The 1 at the left end represents full health and 0 at the right end represents death. It is now possible to use the scale to score different health outcomes.[1]

---

[1] Utilities are frequently obtained using what has been called the *standard reference gamble*. In the standard reference gamble the decision-maker is asked to

1------------------------------------------------------------------0

Full Health                                                                              Death

What do you want to know about an outcome before you can score it on this utility scale? Research on utilities suggest that most people consider at least the following: (1) the type and extent of symptoms that are produced by the outcome; (2) the extent to which the outcome affects the activities of daily living including: mobility, physical activity, professional and social activity and (3) duration of the outcome (i.e., is it temporary or permanent?). Thus, before scoring the utility that results from the side effect of RESTRICT you need more details about the consequences of the side effect of RESTRICT. The side effect of RESTRICT results in the following:

> ■■The muscle destruction caused by RESTRICT produces muscle tightness and pain that totally limits the ability to exercise strenuously. Individuals are able to walk without pain, are able to drive a car, and can perform self care. The restriction does not affect non-athletic professional performance. Those who recover after taking RESTRICT, on average, end up with the muscle strength and tone they would otherwise have 15 years later. Once it has occurred the destruction is permanent, but it does not progress—except as a natural result of aging.   ■■

Can you score this muscle destruction side effect of RESTRICT for yourself on the utility scale which extends from 1 (which equals your state of full health) to 0 (which equals death)? Where on the scale did you place the state of health cre-

choose between a guaranteed state of reduced health and a gamble which includes a probability of full health and a complementary probability of death. The standard gamble thus incorporates an individual's risk-taking tendency, as will be discussed in Chapter 3, as well as their estimate of the utility of the health state itself. In *The Measures of Medicine* we will look at these two phenomena separately. Another alternative method for obtaining utilities is known as the *time trade-off method*.

ated by RESTRICT? Did you place it near 1 because it would have little impact on your life, thus giving it a utility very close to full health or 1? Alternatively, did you give it a much lower utility because it would have a substantial impact on your life?

Estimating utilities in this way sometimes assumes that we are interested in taking into account only those factors that affect us personally. At times we may want to take into account the effect of a particular outcome on others such as family or the community. These impacts may include such factors as the burden of caring for the patient or the potential to spread disease to others. Estimating utilities without considering the impact on others will be called the *personal impact assumption*.[2]

In addition, obtaining utilities in this way assumes that estimates of utilities prior to experiencing an event will not change after the event has been experienced. This assumption will be called the *stability of utilities assumption*. In general it has been found that there is some degree of accommodation or adaptation that occurs after individuals experience a disability. In general utilities estimated prior to experiencing a disability are somewhat lower than those reported after the occurrence of the disability. In other words the utilities of patients who have experienced a condition are generally higher than those of patients or clinicians who have not experienced the condition.

Utilities often differ dramatically between individuals in ways that cannot always be easily predicted. Age often can be a factor because physical disabilities are often viewed as more serious by the young. Differences between men and women and with regard to socioeconomic or ethnic factors are usually small or non existent. As a general rule knowing the average utility for one group allows us to predict the average utility for another group. However, if we want to know about an individual's utility we need to ask them. For some situations it is possible to use average utilities from groups. For instance one might use:

---

[2] The personal impact assumption implies that harm-benefit analysis is usually done from a personal rather than a social perspective. A social perspective would imply that benefits and harms would be included even if they affect other individuals or occurs in subsequent generations. These social impacts will become important when we include cost consideration in Part II.

| Mild angina | .85 |
| Kidney transplant | .84 |
| Severe angina | .70 |
| Home dialysis | .65 |
| Hospital dialysis | .57 |

Utility scales usually set death as zero and do not permit scores less than zero. Nonetheless most individuals can imagine a health state worse than death. For instance, most well adults as well as those who are chronically ill regard a state of coma for the rest of their lives as worse than death. States of constant pain and permanent dementia are also regarded as worse than death by many individuals. It is possible to use a scale in which immediate death is given a utility greater than zero and zero is reserved for a health state worse than immediate death. This approach, however, has rarely been used in decision analysis.

Now let us return to our goal of combining utilities with probabilities. If we use the same scale for measuring utilities as we use for measuring probabilities, then we can combine probabilities and utilities to obtain a measurement which summarizes the results of our decision tree. If we multiply the probability and the utility, we obtain what is called an *expected utility*. For instance if the probability of an outcome is 90% or .9 and the utility of that outcome is .7, then the expected utility is $(.9)(.7) = .63$.

The expected utility is really the probability of an outcome taking into account or adjusting for its quality. If the probability of an outcome is 100% or 1 and the utility of the outcome is full health or 1 then the expected utility is $(1)(1) = 1$. Thus, an expected utility of 1 represents complete assurance of full health. Therefore, 1 is the maximum obtainable or ideal expected utility. When using probabilities and utilities less than 1 we are really comparing our results to the maximum obtainable expected utility or 1. The results of expected utility calculations are measured in a unit which is called a *quality-adjusted life*.[3]

Calculation of expected utility for each potential outcome involves multiplying the outcome's probability by its utility and calculating an expected utility for each potential outcome.

---

[3] Life expectancy can be included in a harm-benefit analysis thereby using quality-adjusted life years rather than quality-adjusted lives as the basic unit of measurement. The use of life expectancy will be discussed in Chapter 5.

The sum of these expected utilities for each of the potential outcomes of a particular treatment option is called the *overall expected utility.* Notice here that we are adding together not only the outcomes that result in cure or other benefits but also the outcomes that result in harm. Outcomes that result in harm often leave an individual with a reduced (but not a 0) utility. Death, however, which carries a utility of 0, results in an expected utility of 0, because 0 multiplied by any probability equals 0.

To obtain the overall expected utility the following calculations are performed:

1. Calculate the path probability for the first potential outcome of a treatment option.
2. Multiply the path probability of that potential outcome of treatment by the utility of that outcome to obtain an expected utility of that potential outcome.
3. Repeat this process calculating the expected utilities of each of the potential outcomes of a treatment option.
4. Add the expected utilities for each of the potential outcomes of a treatment option to obtain the overall expected utility of that treatment option.

Notice that it is the overall expected utility rather than the probabilities of adverse outcomes that we use to summarize the decision tree. Previously we merely added together the probabilities of death or the probabilities of survival. Since death has a utility of 0, an outcome of death also have an expected utility of zero. When an outcome results in reduced quality of health but not death the outcome has an expected utility greater than zero. Thus all outcomes other than death contribute to the overall expected utility.

Probabilities estimate what can be expected to happen and utilities indicate the resulting quality of health. Thus, the overall expected utility indicates the average utility that can be expected from a treatment option measured in a unit called a quality-adjusted life. The maximum quality-adjusted life is equal to 1 and the minimum is zero.

The calculations in the expected utility approach take into account improvements in health that we are calling benefits and reductions in health that we are calling harms. Thus, we can also think of the overall expected utility as summarizing benefits mi-

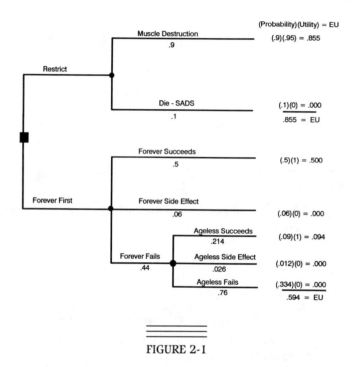

FIGURE 2-1

nus harms or net benefits. Benefits minus harms is also called *effectiveness*.

Expected utilities are so important in quantitative decision-making that this approach to making a decision in a harm-benefit analysis is sometimes called *expected utility theory*. The method used to choose between options is to select the one with the largest overall expected utility. When we use this process of selecting the option with the largest overall expected utility we are aiming to maximize expected utility.

Now let us incorporate measurements of utility into calculation of expected utility and overall expected utility. Let us imagine that for you the side effects of RESTRICT has a utility of .95. We can use your utility to calculate overall expected utilities. Then we will see how we can compare these results to the use of the FOREVER-first approach.

Figure 2-1 demonstrates how probabilities are multiplied by utilities to obtain expected utilities and then how the expected utilities of the potential outcomes of a particular treatment option are added to obtain overall expected utilities. In decision trees we use probabilities from 0 to 1 instead of percentages. Therefore we also use utilities between 0 and 1 instead of between 0 and 100.

Now let us calculate the overall expected utility for the option to use RESTRICT and also the option to use FOREVER-first. For the treatment option to use RESTRICT the steps are as follows:

1. Calculate the path probabilities of each potential outcome. The path probabilities appear as the first column of numbers along the right hand margin of the decision tree. The probability of muscle destruction is .9 and the probability of death from SADS is .1. In other words, everyone who survives develops muscle destruction.

2. Estimate the utility of each of the potential outcomes. These are indicated under the second column along the right hand margin of the decision tree marked utility. The utility of muscle destruction has been set at .95 and the utility of death equals 0.

3. Multiply each of the path probabilities times its corresponding utility to produce an expected utility for each of the potential outcomes. For instance, the expected utility of muscle destruction equals $(.9)(.95) = .855$ and the expected utilities of Die $-$ SADS equal $(.1)(0) = 0$.

4. Add all the expected utilities which may result from a particular treatment option such as the use of RESTRICT. For instance, the overall expected utility for RESTRICT equals $.855 - 0 = .855$.

The overall expected utility of RESTRICT is .855, whereas the overall expected utility of FOREVER-first is .595. Is this an impressive result? Once again we can calculate a number-needed-to-treat to help us evaluate the importance of the results. The number-needed-to-treat which is calculated from a decision tree which includes both probabilities and utilities can be called an *adjusted number-needed-to-treat*. By incorporating utilities the adjusted number needed-to-treat takes into account outcomes in addition to full health and death. The adjusted number-needed-to-treat is calculated in parallel to the calculation of the number-needed-to-treat. Instead of using the probabilities alone it uses overall expected utilities.

Adjusted number-needed-to-treat =

$$\frac{1}{(\text{Overall expected utility of RESTRICT}) - (\text{overall expected utility of FOREVER-first})}$$

$$\text{Adjusted number-needed-to-treat} = \frac{1}{.855 - .594} = 3.8$$

This adjusted number-needed-to-treat tells us that we need to treat 3.8 individuals with RESTRICT, on average, to produce the equivalent of one additional life at full health compared to treating them with FOREVER-first. These lives at full health are actually made up of individuals who would otherwise be dead but who are now living with a utility which has been given a score of .95. Thus for every additional individual who survives because of the use of RESTRICT, .95 of a quality adjusted life is gained.

The expected utility approach makes the assumption that we can add the expected utility of each of the potential outcomes. Thus, we are acting as if adding .1 to the utility of 10 lives is the same as bringing one person to full health who would otherwise be dead (i.e., bringing one person from 0 to 1). Thus, the expected utility approach assumes that expected utility units are all equal and they can therefore be added together. We will call this the *equal utility units* assumption.

This equal utility units assumption implies that the difference between a utility of .1 and a utility of .2 is the same as the difference between a utility of .1 and a utility of 0 (i.e., death). Thus, the equal utility units assumption implies that death is treated as if it were an extension of disability.[4]

The adjusted number-needed-to-treat of 3.8 indicates that if the utility of .95 is accurate and the equal utility units assumption is accepted, the option to use RESTRICT represents a very substantial improvement, it is the clear recommendation of the decision analysis. Another way to look at this result is to realize that if everyone could be brought back to a utility of 1, as is our goal, then

---

[4] Remember that all events are considered permanent and can occur only one time. Thus death is considered a linear extension of other reductions in utility. To the extent that decision-makers regard death as different the expected utility calculation performed on a continuous scale will not reflect their true utilities. (See *The Measures of Medicine* computer program for additional examination of this death effect.)

the overall expected utility would be $(1)(1) = 1$. With RESTRICT we have reached .855 compared with .594 for FOREVER-first. Thus, substantially more of our goal has been achieved.

Is this improvement enough that you would recommend RESTRICT to your patients? It would depend on the utility your patients put on RESTRICT. Thus, the results of our decision tree may depend on the exact utility score used for the outcomes produced by RESTRICT. When there is doubt about the accuracy or stability of the utilities we can use a form of a sensitivity analysis to see if small or modest changes in the utility score alters the recommended treatment of choice.

Individuals differ in how they look at different outcomes; however, there are limits to the range of utilities people place on potential outcomes. For instance, the vast majority of people, except perhaps for professional athletes or dancers, would most likely place the utility of the side effects of RESTRICT somewhere between .70 and .99. Thus, .70 may be regarded as a realistic low estimate and .99 as a realistic high estimate. Now we can calculate an overall expected utility using a .70 utility instead of a .95 utility. Figure 2-2 displays the results of the decision analysis. Notice that even with a utility of .7, RESTRICT has a greater expected utility than FOREVER-first.

On the basis of this decision analysis it is reasonable for clinicians to recommend RESTRICT to most patients. Before we make this recommendation, however, we need to let the patient know about the side effects of RESTRICT. Patients need an opportunity to tell us that for them the outcome of RESTRICT is a terrible thing with utilities well below .70. Generally, however, it may be reasonable to recommend RESTRICT on the basis of the information contained in this decision analysis.

Thus, we can often make best guesses at the utilities and then try to estimate a realistic high and a realistic low estimate that we believe represents the likely range of utilities. A sensitivity analysis can then be performed to determine if the recommendation would be changed if the utility was closer to the realistic high or realistic low estimate. If the recommendation changes based on changes in utility within this realistic range, the patient's own utility need to be incorporated into the decision analysis early in the process before calculating the overall expected utilities. In these circumstances, our recommendation will go one way or the other based on an individual patient's own utility.

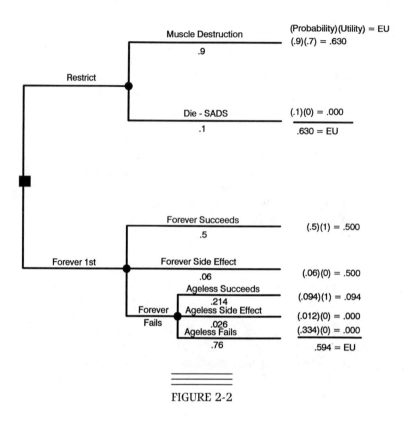

FIGURE 2-2

Now we have examined how we can measure utilities and combine them with probabilities to obtain expected utilities and overall expected utilities. We have also performed a sensitivity analysis to examine whether our recommendations are likely to change depending on the utility scores used. In performing these calculations we assumed that we had accurate information on all the potential outcomes. As we will see now this is not always the case.

■One day several months later after ordering a routine RE-STRICT prescription for one of your patients you receive a warning message. The message says that on the basis of the first 200,000 prescriptions for RESTRICT, WISH has concluded that RESTRICT is the cause of irreversible blindness with a probability of 1 per 1,000 or .001.

Why, you wonder, was this side effect not recognized before WISH approved RESTRICT. The message continues saying that prior to approval 1,500 individuals had received RESTRICT and no cases of blindness had occurred. WISH had concluded that a rare but serious side effect was still possible which is why they had recommended the use of RESTRICT initially only for those who refused other treatment.■■

RESTRICT had been administered to 1,500 patients and blindness had not occurred yet now they are saying that blindness occurs with a probability of 1 per 1,000 and that they knew all along that this was possible. WISH was relying on the *rule of 3*. The rule of 3 indicates how may individuals need to receive a treatment before we can be 95% confident that at least one case of the side effect will be observed. To be 95% confident of observing at least one case of blindness, if the probability of blindness is 1 per 1,000, it is necessary to include 3,000 individuals in the group receiving RESTRICT. That is, to be 95% confident of observing at least one case of the side effect, we must observe 3 times the reciprocal of the true probability of the side effects or:

$$(3) \; \frac{(1)}{(.001)} = 3000$$

The fact that there were no cases of blindness or other rare but serious side effects in the first 1500 patients thus did not provide great assurance that no rare but serious harm could occur.[5]

**DOES THIS NEW INFORMATION ALTER YOUR DECISION WHETHER OR NOT TO RECOMMEND RESTRICT?**

[5] Using the rule of 3 in reverse it is possible to draw a tentative conclusion from the 1500 individuals who initially received the treatment without any cases of blindness. We can say with 95% confidence that if a rare but serious side effect like blindness occurs it occurs with a probability of 3 per 1,500 or less. That is, we should still expect previously unrecognized side effects to appear which have a probability of 1 per 500 (0.2%) or less. Thus, to discover that blindness which actually occurs with a frequency of 1 per 1,000 was not initially observed should not be surprising.

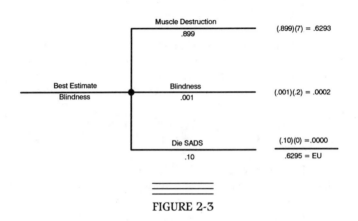

FIGURE 2-3

Blindness can be added to our decision tree to find out whether it changes the recommendation. We already know the probability of blindness according to WISH (i.e., .001) but what about the utility of blindness. Data in the literature may suggest that, on average, blindness is regarded as having a utility of approximately .40. However, you may want to start by asking your particular patient. These patients need to be informed anyway about this new information. Asking your patients is feasible because they know exactly what you mean by blindness; answering, however, may be difficult for them. They may have never spent time with blind people and cannot imagine how it affects their daily lives. When you ask a patient they may say "somewhere between .80 and .20."

This may not seem very satisfying to you but it's the best they can do. Therefore, let us use this range of utilities in our decision analysis. We are again performing a type of sensitivity analysis to determine whether the range of potential utilities alters the recommendation of the decision analysis. Our aim is to determine whether adding blindness to the decision analysis reduces the overall expected utility of RESTRICT below that of FOREVER-first. Therefore we will use the patient's low estimate of the utility of blindness of .2.

Figure 2-3 displays the use of RESTRICT, including irreversible blindness. The overall expected utility of RESTRICT is now

.6295, instead of .6300 when blindness was omitted from the decision tree as in Figure 2-2. This is a very small difference because blindness is very unusual.

WISH was wrong about the probability of blindness before; perhaps they have still underestimated the probability of developing blindness. What are the implications if the probability is much higher? To assess the potential impact of a much higher probability of blindness we can perform what is sometimes called *a worst-case analysis*. A worst-case analysis is a special type of sensitivity analysis. It doesn't really assess the worst possible situation. Rather it uses two or more realistic high or realistic low estimates and recalculates the overall expected utility.

A worst-case analysis for blindness can be performed by incorporating a realistic high estimate of the probability and combining this with our realistic low estimate for the utility of blindness. This new result can then be compared to the overall expected utility of FOREVER-first. WISH has estimated the probability of blindness to be 1 per 1,000 on the basis of the first 200,000 prescriptions. That is a large number of prescriptions but still leaves room for doubt. It is hard to image, based on the number of prescriptions for RESTRICT, the probability of blindness being more than 1 per 100 or .01. Thus, .01 can be used as our realistic high estimate for blindness.

Figure 2-4 displays part of the decision tree for our worst-case sensitivity analysis for RESTRICT with the probability of blindness set at .01, the utility of blindness set at .2, and the utility of the muscle destruction side effect set at .7. The overall expected utility of RESTRICT is now .6250 compared with its previous level of .6295. Remember the overall expected utility of FOREVER-first is .5940. The results are moving slightly closer but even the worst-case analysis recommends RESTRICT on the basis of the overall expected utilities. In fact even if we made blindness equal to death and thus, gave it a given utility of 0, RESTRICT would still have a higher overall expected utility (.6230) than FOREVER-first (.5940).

Thus, our decision analysis has produced some useful information. Patients need to know this new information about the potential for blindness; they also need to know that the situation has been carefully analyzed and RESTRICT can still be recommended.

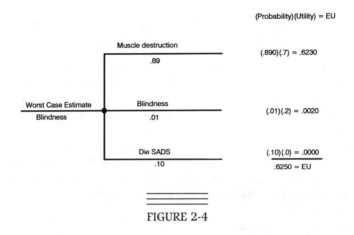

FIGURE 2-4

We have now learned to incorporate utilities into our decision making. However, up until now we have continued to assume that all of the potential outcomes will occur immediately. As we will see now this is not always the case and we need to take into account the timing of the harms and of the benefits.

## TIMING

Thus far, we have been acting as if outcomes of a therapy occur immediately. This simplification allowed us to avoid the difficult question of how valuable current health is compared with future health. However, as we will now see outcomes may take time to occur and we are forced to consider the timing of benefits and harms.

As the SADS epidemic continues the world-wide research effort against SADS produces an important new advance. By analyzing the SOY cells it is now possible to accurately predict the chances of developing SADS during the next year.

In addition a new treatment has been approved that will

delay the onset of SADS. The drug called ONE-AND-ONLY
has been approved for one year of treatment only because its severe side effects occur only after one year of use. Unfortunately
the studies have demonstrated that during the first year and
only the first year after completion of a year of ONE-AND-
ONLY the chances of developing SADS actually increase compared to the chances if ONE-AND-ONLY had not been given.

The exact chances of developing SADS during the first
year after completing a 1 year course of ONE-AND-ONLY
have not been established. However, for your patient who has
a 20% chance of developing SADS during the next year the
chances of developing SADS the first year off ONE-AND-
ONLY is somewhere between 22% and 40%.                    ▬

Everything else being equal almost everyone would prefer a
treatment that delays SADS one year compared to a treatment
which allows SADS to develop in the immediate future. That is,
harms in the more distant future are not generally considered as
bad as harm in the immediate future. The harder question is how
strong is this preference for current health benefits? How can we
measure the strength of this preference for current health compared to future health?

One way to measure how strongly current benefits are fa-
vored is to see how much you are willing to increase your probability of developing SADS in the future in exchange for assurance
that it will not develop during the next year. On the basis of this
personal assessment of the value of current health, compared to
future health let us see what you would recommend to patients
depending on different probabilities of developing SADS during
the year after ONE-AND-ONLY is stopped?

▬▬In each of the following choices (A through D), would you
recommend #1 or #2?

(A)
  #1.    Refuse therapy and accept the 20% chance of develop-
         ing SADS during the next year.

> #2.   Choose the therapy and accept a 22% chance of devel-
>        oping SADS during the first year after completing a 1
>        year course of ONE-AND-ONLY.
>
> (B)
>   #1.   Refuse the therapy and accept the 20% chance of de-
>         veloping SADS during the next year.
>   #2.   Choose the therapy and accept a 25% chance of devel-
>         oping SADS during the first year after completing a 1
>         year course of ONE-AND-ONLY.
>
> (C)
>   #1.   Refuse the therapy and accept the 20% chance of de-
>         veloping SADS during the next year.
>   #2.   Choose the therapy and accept a 30% chance of devel-
>         oping SADS during the first year after completing a 1
>         year course of ONE-AND-ONLY.
>
> (D)
>   #1.   Refuse the therapy and accept the 20% chance of de-
>         veloping SADS during the next year.
>   #2.   Choose the therapy and accept a 40% chance of devel-
>         oping SADS during the first year after completing a 1
>         year course of ONE-AND-ONLY.   ▬

By choosing the treatment you are recommending that the patient accept a greater benefit now in return for a greater harm
later. The higher the probability you ask them to accept for development of SADS in the future, the more importance you are
placing on time in the immediate future. This is called *discounting*
or giving less importance to harms and benefits which occur in
the future. If treatment is always chosen then the discount for the
year gained is greater than 100% because you were willing to
increase your probability of developing SADS from .2 to .4 in
order to be assured of not developing SADS during the next year.

If you eventually recommended that ONE-AND-ONLY be
refused as the probability of future SADS increased, the discount
for the year gained can be estimated. Depending on which question you first recommended that ONE-AND-ONLY be refused, the discount for the year gained is:

A—less than 10%
B—between 10% and 25%

C—between 25% and 50%
D—between 50% and 100%

Whenever harms and benefits do not occur at the same time, discounting is an issue. Most people place a high value on time in the immediate future. This may be especially true for severely ill individuals if it allows them to get their affairs in order, to see friends or family, or to make a special trip. Thus, patients often exhibit a special preference for time in the immediate future. In addition, when medical advances are occurring rapidly, extra time provides hope that a new advance will make the outlook better.

Time after the immediate future (for instance after one year) tends to carry a lower value. Living one year may seem like half as long as two years to a few people but to most that first year will be worth much more than the second year. However, it is important to recognize that once the first year is nearing an end, the second year's value to the individual will often increase dramatically perhaps causing them to regret their previous decision.

At the other extreme, time in the distant future may have a very low value to some patients. The patient who does not want to live "too long" who does not want to become a burden for others, may actually be saying that beyond a certain age or a certain state of health they actually prefer death to life.

Discounting is not always separately included in a harm-benefit analysis or included in a decision tree. Discounting for time may be incorporated into assessment of utility. A benefit which does not occur for many years may not be perceived as having as high a utility as a benefit which occurs immediately. Similarly a harm which occurs in the distant future may reduce the utility less compared to a harm that may occur soon in the immediate future.

When discounting for harms or benefits that occur in the future is not performed or is not incorporated into the assessment of utilities another assumption is being made. It is then assumed that the benefits and harms occur immediately. Alternatively, the assumption may be made that harms which occur in the future are valued the same as harms which occurred immediately and benefits which occur in the future are valued the same as benefits which occur in the future. Because this is not usually true, we need to be aware of the timing of benefits and harms.

Now we have completed our look at the basic steps which go into analyzing harms and benefits using the decision tree approach to decision analysis. We have learned to measure and compare probabilities and to incorporate utilities and timing of the potential outcomes into our recommendations. We have learned that we can now make recommendations based on the alternative with the greatest overall expected utility. Unfortunately, we may find that the recommendations we make based on expected utilities are not always greeted with universal approval. Thus now we need to turn our attention to how and why clinicians and patients may wish to deviated from recommendations based on expected utilities.

# CHAPTER THREE

# Risk-Taking and Risk-Avoiding

Thus far, our decisions have been based on the principle that the best choice among options is the one with the largest overall expected utility. In obtaining expected utilities we focused entirely on the probabilities, the utilities, and perhaps the timing of the potential outcomes. We ignored important considerations that tend to be incorporated into the actual decision-making process. At times all of us select alternatives which deviate from the choices which are recommended by expected utility. When we deviate from the recommendation of expected utility, we are said to be *risk-taking* or *risk-avoiding*.[1]

Advocates of the expected utility approach to decision-making have at times defined decisions made on the basis of the largest expected utility as "rational" leaving the impression that the frequent deviations from the recommendations of expected

---

[1] The term risk is very confusing because it has other meanings. At times it is equated with harms, and the form of analysis that we are calling harm-benefit analysis is called risk-benefit analysis. This use of risk will not be used in *The Measures of Medicine*. At other times it is equated with probability as is often the case in statistical terminology. When risk is used alone in *The Measures of Medicine* it implies a probability.

utility are irrational. Because of the frequency of our risk-taking and risk-avoiding it is important that we understand the common situations in which they occur.

We often deviate from the choices recommended by expected utility in ways that are quite predictable. In these situations the vast majority of people deviate in the same direction perhaps varying only in the degree to which they deviate. At other times there are individual differences; with some people deviating in one direction and some in the opposite direction.[2]

These deviations from expected utility are the result of both our attitudes toward the decision and the way the choices are presented. Thus we will take a look at a series of causes of deviations from expected utility which are the result of attitudes and presentations.

---

## ATTITUDES

To illustrate risk-taking or risk-avoiding attitudes we will return to a series of choices related to the SADS epidemic. In looking at these deviations from the recommendations of expected utility you will hopefully learn about you own personal tendencies. As you make your choices respond as if you were making these choices for yourself and not as if you were making a recommendation for a patient.

Imagine that SADS and previous treatments have left you with a quality of health equivalent to .8 compared with your previous quality of full health (i.e., = 1). Imagine that you are offered the following pair of options but you can select only one of the two options (#1 or #2) from each pair.

[2] In theory it is possible to incorporate these deviations from expected utility into the quantitative decision-making process by giving additional weights to particular probabilities or utilities. This weighting process is rarely performed as part of decision analysis and is not illustrated in *The Measures of Medicine*. However, the standard reference gamble method of assessing utilities incorporates one aspect of risk-avoiding, or what we will call the *certainty effect*. Deviations from expected utility here imply deviations from expected utility performed without a weighting process.

> Which one of the two options (#1 or #2) do you prefer?
> (Make your choice before looking at the decision trees.)
>
> #1. Select a treatment with the following possible out-
> comes: 50% chance of raising the quality of your health
> from .8 to 1. 50% chance of an outcome that reduces
> the quality of your health from .8 to .6.
>
> #2. Refuse the treatment and accept a quality of your health
> of .8. ▬

Which answer did you choose? Did you select #1 because to
you a quality of health of .8 is a severe reduction and well worth
the possibility of a further reduction in return for the equally large
probability of obtaining your previous full state of health? Alternatively, did you conclude that the status quo with a quality of health
of .8 is a modest and manageable reduction and is apparently a certainty or guarantee that your health will not be reduced further?

Figure 3-1 displays the choices in the form of a decision tree.
Notice that the two options have equal expected utility, and thus
they are a toss-up according to expected utility theory. Neither
choice is considered better than the other. Option #2 has only
one branch because by selecting the status quo there is only one
potential outcome which therefore is a certainty and carries a
probability of 1 (i.e., 100%).

In the situations faced so far the probabilities have always
been less than 1. Thus there was always chance involved in
determining which outcome would occur. This was always indicated in our decision tree by a circle or chance node which had
two or more branches. Many decisions involve probabilities less
than 1. However, when one of the choices is to accept the status
quo, we may be assuming that the probability of the status quo
continuing is equal to 1; we often think and act as if the situation
will remain the same. Thus, we think and act as if we have a
guarantee. This guarantee or certainty effect can alter our atti-
tude toward our options.[3]

---

[3] The literature often refers to this guarantee effect as an uncertainty effect.
Unfortunately the term uncertainty has two very different meanings. It can
refer to the unknown outcome that inevitably results from probabilities. In
addition, uncertainty can refer to the additional unknown that results from

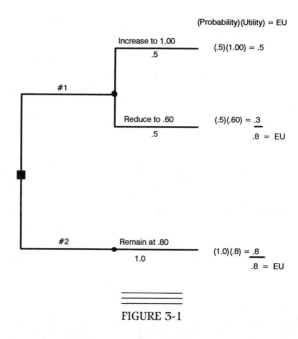

FIGURE 3-1

Many individuals confronted with this toss–up choice select option #2 because they are influenced by the guarantee effect. In general we tend to favor retaining the status quo when we feel we can tolerate the current state of health and believe it will continue. When this occurs, we are said to be *risk-aversive*. In health care, however, there are many times when the current situation is not tolerable or when it is clear that an individual's health is deteriorating and will continue do so. The next set of choices may pose this type of situation.

---

▄▄▄Imagine that the quality of your health has been severely impaired. The quality of your health has been reduced to .2. Imagine you are offered the following pair of options but you can select only one of the two options (#1 or #2)
Which one of the two options (#1 or #2) do you prefer?

ambiguity: that is, the imprecision of our estimates of probabilities. The guarantee or certainty effect refers to the unknown which results from probabilities. We will also discuss later in this chapter the ambiguity effect.

#1.  Select a treatment with the following possible outcomes:
5% chance of raising the quality to your health from .2 to 1.
55% chance of leaving the quality of your health at .2.
40% chance of reducing the quality to your heath from .2 to .1.

#2.  Refuse the treatment and accept a quality of your health equal to .2. ▬

Figure 3-2 displays the options #1 and #2. Again the options have the same expected utility and would be considered a toss-up according to decision analysis. However, for most people a quality of health equal to .2 is so bad that they are willing to take a substantial chance of a further reduction to have even a low probability of obtaining a desired state of health. In this situation a guaranteed outcome such as remaining at the current state of health may look very undesirable. In these situations we often favor a gamble over a guarantee. We will call this common phenomenon the *long-shot effect.*

The long-shot effect and the guarantee effect work in opposite directions. The guarantee effect encourages us to accept the current state of health or the status quo while the long-shot effect encourages us to reject the status quo and take a gamble.

The long-shot effect may have a very strong influence on the decisions of clinicians and patients. As conditions deteriorate, patients and clinicians may feel that there is very little to lose and may be willing to go after a gamble even when decisions based on expected utility clearly favor no treatment or different treatment. The following choice examines the consequences of the long-shot effect.

▬Again imagine that the quality of your health has been severely impaired. The quality of your health has been reduced to .2. Imagine that you are offered the following pair of options but you can select only one of the two options (#1 or #2). Which of the two options (#1 or #2) do you prefer?

> #1. Select a treatment with the following possible outcomes:
> 1% chance of raising the quality to your health from .2 to 1.
> 55% chance of leaving the quality of your health at .2.
> 44% chance of reducing the quality to your heath from .2 to .1.
>
> #2. Refuse the treatment and accept a quality of your health equal to .2. ▄▄▄

Figure 3-3 displays the results of these options. Option #2, the status quo, is clearly the best option as judged by expected utilities. The adjusted number-needed-to-treat comparing option #2 to option #1 is approximately 28 suggesting that accepting the status quo with a quality of health of .2 is the clear recommendation of expected utility theory. Did you agree? If not would you change your mind now? Clinicians and patients often select a treatment even after knowing that it is clearly inferior according to expected utility theory.

How far would you go? Would you choose to take the treatment if there is a 0.5% chance of raising the quality of your

FIGURE 3-2

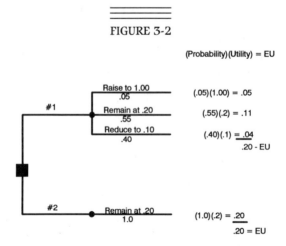

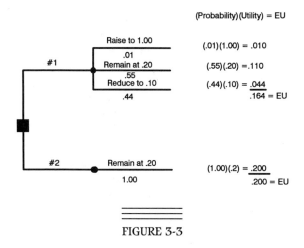

(Probability)(Utility) = EU

Raise to 1.00    (.01)(1.00) = .010

.01

#1    Remain at .20    (.55)(.20) =.110

.55

Reduce to .10    (.44)(.10) = .044

.44    .164 = EU

#2    Remain at .20    (1.00)(.2) = .200

1.00    .200 = EU

FIGURE 3-3

health to 1? What if there is 0.1% or 1 in a thousand chance? Is there a point where you would regard the probability of success as so low that you would accept the status quo believing that treatment is futile?

Many patients and some clinicians favor decisions with a 1% or lower chance of improving a poor quality of health even when expected utilities favor no treatment. At its extreme the long-shot effect means that patients may prefer treatments with such low probabilities of success that most outside observers would label them as futile.[4]

Thus, if a patient's current health state or status quo is intolerable they may look at risk-taking very differently compared to when their current health state or status quo is quite tolerable. Thus, it is important to assess how an individual views their status quo in order to determine whether they will tend to favor a treatment or alternatively favor acceptance of the status quo.

An individual's perception of benefits and harms, however, may not use their current state of health or the status

---

[4] Thus, there is a danger in leaving decision making entirely to the individual patient. In theory clinicians do not have an obligation to offer options which are considered futile. As these exercises suggest, it is difficult to define what futile means because those who see themselves as living in an unacceptable state will choose almost any long-shot.

quo as the point of reference for making decisions. Losses and gains are often viewed from the individual's own previous experience. An individual's previous health status, or one to which they aspire, may set what is called their *reference point*. They may set their reference point as perfect health allowing them to again compete in athletics or take full responsibilities for care of their family. They may set their reference point based on a sought after cosmetic improvement. They may also set their reference point aiming to avoid the side effect they suffered during earlier treatment. Understanding an individual's hopes and aspirations and therefore their reference point is key to understanding what they seek as a gain and what they avoid as a loss.

The guarantee effect and the long-shot effect are likely to operate on all of us to one degree or another. Individuals may vary as to the strength of these effects. However, understanding an individual's goals and fears and therefore their reference point can help us appreciate which effect is likely to be dominant. For instance, individuals in a newly developed state of poor health are likely to be influenced by the long-shot effect. They become risk-takers as they aspire to improve their health. Individuals with long-standing stable disabilities may be influenced by the guarantee effect. They may become risk-aversive as they confront the possibility of further reducing their quality of health.

Two individuals may find themselves in what to the outside observer looks like identical circumstances with identical choices. Yet they may look at the potential outcomes very differently. One may regard the potential improvement offered by a therapy as a loss relative to their previous or hoped for state of health; the other may regard the same outcome as a gain relative to their current health state. Losses or gains then depend on your perspective or reference point.

The guarantee and the long-shot effect are not the only factors which influence our risk-taking attitudes. Another phenomenon known as *regret and responsibility* strongly influence our choices. Regret and responsibility comes into play when one of the options is perceived to place greater responsibility on the shoulders of the decision-maker than another option. The influence which responsibility and the resulting regret may have on your decisions is illustrated in the next decision.

---

■■Which one of the two situations (#1 or #2) do you prefer?

#1.    You are treating a patient who has SADS with drug A. You have considered switching to drug B but decided against it. You and your patient now find out that she would have been better off if you had switched to drug B.

#2.    You had been treating a patient who has SADS with drug B but you switched the patient to drug A. You and your patient now find out that she would have been better off if she had remained on drug B.    ■■

---

Most people select option #1. These two situation are the same except that in option #1 an active role was not taken. This type of error is known as an *error of omission*. In option #2 the outcome is the same, but an active intervention occurred. This type of error is known as an *error of commission*.

Are errors of commission worse than errors of omission? In general when given a choice between these two options individuals favor errors of omission. Errors of omission may not carry the same degree of regret or the same degree of responsibility. Expected utility does not distinguish between errors of omission and errors of commission, however, in societies where these are viewed as different, this distinction may well affect the decision-making of clinicians and sometimes of patients.[5]

In addition to influencing our choices for any one patient, issues of responsibility can influence how we make decisions when allocated limited resources between patients. For instance imagine the choice between these two approaches to treating SADS.

---

■■A new approach to treating SADS has been developed using SOY cell transplantation. Individuals who receive SOY cell transplants have an 80% chance of success on the first attempt

---

[5] Many experts in bioethics regard errors of omission and errors of commission as ethically the same. To the extent however that legally and psychologically they are regarded as different they are likely to remain important determinants of decision-making.

with a matched donor and a 60% chance of success on the second attempt. You have recently become an expert in performing SOY cell transplants.

You have been following a patient for several years and watched their SOY cells slowly fail despite your efforts to provide the best and latest treatment available. You perform a SOY cell transplant which you and the patient optimistically view as their best hope. Unfortunately despite using your best technique, the SOY cell transplant fails on the first attempt. A large number of patients are seeking your services for their first SOY cell transplant.

Which one of the two options (#1 or #2) do you prefer?

#1.  Make a second attempt at SOY cell transplant in your long standing patient who failed the first transplant.

#2.  Provide a first attempt at SOY cell transplant in a new patient recently referred to you. ▬

Despite the increased chance of a good outcome for the first-time recipient of a SOY cell transplant, it is difficult to refuse your long-standing patient. Your involvement in the first attempt and your sense of responsibility may make this a difficult choice even though the probabilities are clearly in favor of providing the transplant to the new unknown patient.

Issues of regret and responsibility color a great number of clinical decisions. Because of the concern for regret and responsibility, physicians may have greater concerns about iatrogenic side effects than bad outcomes which are produced by the disease itself. This tendency to favor errors of omission over errors of commission may explain physicians' tendencies to under anticoagulate, preferring a recurrent pulmonary emboli to a doctor-induced bleed and to keep serum levels of nephrotoxic antibiotics less than therapeutic, rather than taking a chance of producing renal disease.

The effect of regret and responsibility can effect more than how we view the future it can effect how we view the past. Expected utility theory tells us to base future decisions exclusively on their future consequences without taking into account past decisions or past results. Often, however, we take into account past losses hoping to recover from our losses based on current decisions. For instance when a patient has deteriorated as a result of our past treatment we may regard these past losses as past commitments which need to be removed by future successes.[6]

There may be a natural tendency to deviate from the recommendation of expected utility and to include these past commitments in our decision-making process. Regarding past commitments as losses that need to be overcome by future gain, however, can lead us to escalate our commitments and favor choices that we would not favor otherwise. Thus, when our decisions have not gone well it is especially important to step back and treat current choices as new choices (i.e., as separate decisions). It is also an especially good time to seek the advice of others who can be more objective.

Expected utility theory does not take into account past experience, current risk-taking tendencies, or future regret. Benefits or harms of the same magnitude are treated the same. Expected utilities do not even recognize the existence of a gamble or a guarantee. Thus, when performing expected utility calculation we often make the assumption that our attitudes do not influence the decision one way or the other. However, when looking at the recommendations of decision analysis, we need to recognize that our attitudes do in reality influence our decisions.

━━━

## PRESENTATION OF THE DECISION

The choice between treatments, especially close calls or toss-ups, can be influenced not only by the clinician's and the patient's attitudes but also by how and to whom the options are presented. Three issues of presentation of decisions have an especially strong impact on decision making. These are (1) Framing, (2) Ambiguity, and (3) Control.

Let us examine how the presentations of the decision can influence decision making.

---

[6] These past commitments are often called *sunk costs*. The term sunk costs will not be used in discussing harms and benefits in *The Measures of Medicine* because it has a financial implication that is not intended here.

---

■■■Imagine that you have just developed complications of SADS.
Which one of the following treatments do you prefer?

#1.    Treatment A—You will undergo a procedure which car-
       ries a 10% probability of death in the immediate future.
       If you survive the procedure you have a 40% chance of
       dying from SADS in the immediate future.

#2.    Treatment B—You will undergo a procedure and you
       have a 90% chance of surviving the procedure. After
       surviving the procedure you then have a 60% chance of
       complete recovery.                                         ■■■

---

The two options produce the same expected utility. The
majority of individuals, however, will select #2 option. Treatment B is presented in terms of survival whereas treatment A is
presented in terms of death. Thus, treatment B is framed optimistically or positively. Treatment A, in contrast, is presented in
terms of the probability of death, and is framed pessimistically or
negatively.

It is a common clinical phenomenon that decisions presented
optimistically in term of the chances of good outcomes are
viewed more favorably than identical options presented pessimistically in terms of the chances of bad outcomes. That is the
choice is influenced by the way the decision is framed. To avoid
influencing patients by the way the options are framed, it is often
useful to present the same data both ways, for instance, providing the chances for survival and also the chances for death.

Framing may also influence decision-making when it is used
to raise or lower expectations. Whether we regard an outcome as
a loss or a gain can be influenced by the way the outcome is
presented. When we have high expectations of a good outcome
anything less than our expectations may be perceived as a loss.
Lowering expectations so that performance exceeds expectations
can become a fine-tuned art. As clinicians we may find ourselves
practicing subtle deceptions by "hanging crepe"—preparing for
the worst so that the outcome can exceed expectations.

A second basic influence of the way information is presented
depends on the degree of ambiguity or authority conveyed. This
is illustrated in the next decision.

---

■■■Imagine that you have been diagnosed with SADS.
Which one of the two options (#1 or #2) would you select?

#1.   Select a treatment with the following possible out-
      comes:
      50% chance of raising the quality of your health to 1
      and;
      50% chance of reducing the quality of your health to .6.

#2.   Select a treatment with the following possible out-
      comes:
      Somewhere between a 40% and 60% chance of raising
      the quality of your health to 1 and;
      Somewhere between a 40% and 60% chance of reduc-
      ing the quality of your health to .6.          ■■■

---

On average, option #1 and option #2 are equal yet they
may appear quite different. Option #1 is presented as a definite
probability, whereas option #2 is presented as an ambiguous
spread of potential probabilities. Ambiguity is a special form of
uncertainty. Probabilities themselves indicate that we are dealing
with uncertainty. Ambiguity implies that the exact probabilities
are not known.[7]

Everything else being equal most people tend to avoid ambiguity. Thus presenting one option as ambiguous and another as
definitive is likely to favor the more definitive or authoritative
presentation. However, for some people this effect will work the
opposite way. Patients and clinicians may see ambiguity as work-
ing in their favor. Clinicians may say to themselves or to patients
"in my hands the results are better." The patient may respond to
ambiguity by saying "The better probabilities apply to me, I can
beat the averages." Patients or clinicians may feel they can do
better than the average individual because they have control in
implementing a treatment or because they consider their prognosis better than the statistics would suggest.

---

[7] Ambiguity can be taken into account in a decision analysis using a sensitivity
analysis. Sensitivity analysis usually uses realistic high and low estimates
rather than 95% confidence intervals. In decision analysis ambiguity is dealt
with by first denying it exists and then performing a sensitivity analysis to
measure its effect.

A third and key aspect of how the manner of presentation affects decision-making relates to who is in control of the process. The process of informed consent has clearly placed most final decisions in the hands of patients. Patients will often voluntarily choose an option that includes a probability of harm through the process of informed consent. Potential harms that are not voluntarily accepted may be viewed as unacceptable.

The desire for control over the decision making process can be very strong; for instance consider the following options.

---

Imagine that you have developed SADS and now have an undiagnosed life threatening complication. There is a 60% chance that you have complication A and a 40% chance that you have complication B.

Which one of the two options (#1 or #2) would you select?

#1.   A treatment which has 60% chance of cure if you have complication A or complication B.

#2.   A treatment which has a 100% chance of cure if you have complication A.

---

Many people favor option #2 despite the fact that both of these options cure 60% of the complications. This phenomenon has been called *pseudo-control*. It implies that the desire for control can be so strong that we may have an illusion of control even when no real control is possible. Pseudo-control may be used to encourage one choice of options over another. For instance, imagine this type of presentation: "if you choose option #2 and we find complication A, we can cure you; or you can choose option #1 and take your chances." This form of presentation encourages a choice that falsely appears to expand the patient's control.[8]

---

[8] This form of deviation from expected utility has also been called pseudocertainty because 100% provides a false sense that there is no chance of a bad outcome.

Despite the increasing acceptance of informed consent a sub-stantial degree of control over the process remains with the clini-cian. Patients' decisions may be influenced by the degree of control which clinicians have over the process. Surgical options, for instance, often give a greater degree of control to the clinician who performs the procedure compared to medication options. Similarly, in-patient treatment tends to provide a greater degree of control to clinicians, compared with out-patient treatments.[9]

The need for a sense of control differs from person to per-son. Some people prefer driving a car to flying in an airplane because of the sense of control over the process. Treatment that involves the patient in implementation may be important to pa-tients who seeks a greater sense of control. Some patients, how-ever, resist the responsibility that goes along with control and thus favor treatment options that return the responsibility to the clinician. Thus, in looking at the decision-making process it is important to recognize both who controls the treatment and how the control alters the decision-making preference.

Patients differ in the degree to which they wish to control the process. Clinicians, in contrast, tend to prefer options that are under their control. Thus, clinicians may consciously or un-consciously convey these preferences to patients by the way the options are presented.

The expected utility approach to decision-making does not take into account the effects of how the options are presented. When harm-benefit analysis is performed based exclusively upon expected utilities without taking into account the manner of pre-sentation an additional assumption is made; the manner of presen-tation does not affect the decision. The care which is taken in presenting information can minimize—but not eliminate—these effects.

Attitudes can influence decision-making. In addition, the manner of presentation can affect decision-making. The ex-pected-utility calculations of decision analysis do not generally take these factors into consideration. We need to recognize the potential importance of these attitudes and presentations before

---

[9] Control can have other influences on decision making. Voluntary acceptance of the treatment and control over implementation may increase the perceived probability of benefit and reduce the perceived probability of harm. This ef-fect may be especially strong for treatments in which the outcome is generally favorable, so that harms are rarely encountered.

accepting the recommendations of a decision analysis based on expected utilities alone.

Thus, it is not surprising to find that most decision-makers will at times deviate from the recommendations of expected utility theory. This will occur even if the decision-maker agrees with the probabilities and the utilities that have been included when calculating the expected utility. Thus to deviate from the recommendations of expected utility is not irrational, but routine.

In addition to our attitudes and the manner of presentation, our choice may be influenced by the process we actually use in making decisions. Thus in the next chapter we will turn our attention to the processes we use in making decisions.

# CHAPTER FOUR

## Making Choices: Beyond Maximizing Expected Utility

The recommendations of expected utility theory are based on the assumption that our goal is to maximize expected utility. However, even when two options have equal expected utility, we may favor one option over the other.

Let us return to the SADS epidemic to examine other factors that influence our decisions.

---

■Three new approaches are available for combating the SADS epidemic. You may select none, one, two, or all three of these approaches.

Situation A:

You have a 4% chance of developing SADS in the near future. If you develop the disease, there will be a 10% chance that you will die during the acute phase. If you survive the acute phase you will completely recover.

A therapy is available which if used before exposure reduces your chances of developing SADS to 2%. If you develop the disease there is still a 10% chance that you will die during the acute phase. However, a side effect of the therapy causes death in the near future in 0.2% of the people who receive the therapy.

The following two options are available. Check which one of the two options (#1 or #2) you would select:

#1.    Choose to take the therapy.

#2.    Choose not to take the therapy.

Situation B:

Even before your choice on the previous question can be implemented you have been exposed to SADS. Now there is a 40% chance that you will develop the disease in the near future. If you develop the disease there will be a 10% chance that you will die in the near future. If you survive the acute phase, you will completely recover.

A therapy is available that reduces your chances of developing SADS to 20%. If you develop SADS there is still a 10% chance that you will die in the near future. If you survive the acute phase you will completely recover. However, a side effect of the therapy causes death in the near future in 2% of the people who receive the therapy.

The following two options are available to you. Check which one of the two options (#1 or #2) you would select:

#1.    Choose to take the therapy.

#2.    Choose not to take the therapy.

Situation C:

Now imagine that you have developed early SADS but you have no symptoms now. There is a 40% chance of developing SADS with complications and a 25% chance of death in the near future if SADS with complications occurs. If complications do not develop or if you survive the complications, complete recovery will occur.

A therapy is available that reduces your chances of developing complications from 40% to 32%. There is still a 25% chance of death in the near future if complications occur. However, the therapy requires a procedure that itself causes death in the near future 2% of the time.

The following two options are available to you. Check which one of the following two options (#1 or #2) you would select:

#1.    Choose to take the therapy.

#2.    Choose not to take the therapy.

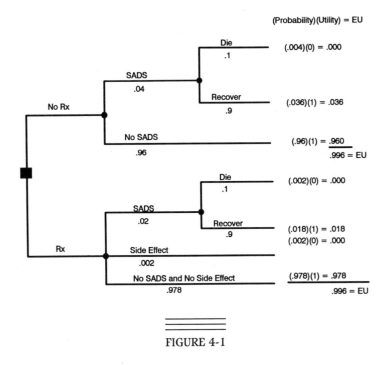

FIGURE 4-1

Figures 4-1, 4-2, and 4-3 display the decision trees for situations A, B, and C respectively. In each situation, the expected utility of #1 and #2 are the same. Thus, according to these decision analyses these options are toss-ups. A toss-up should be a very close and difficult decision. Expected utility theory says that it does not make any difference which decision you choose when confronted with a toss-up.

If these were close and difficult decisions then you may be making decisions using the maximize expected utility principle. In each of these situations most decision-makers have a clear preference despite the fact that these decisions are a toss-up according to their expected utilities. The decision to take or not to take treatment in these three situations is affected by your tendencies to take action. That is, you may use a decision principle that states: treat unless there is a convincing reason not to treat. Alternatively you may use a decision principle that states: do not treat unless there is a convincing reason to treat.

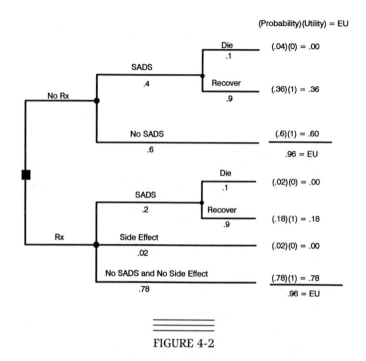

FIGURE 4-2

Some individuals select to take treatment in all three situations; therefore, they deviate from expected utility in a consistent and predictable direction. These people have been said to have a *bias toward action*. They tend to prefer active treatment to observing the natural course of events, even when the two options are equal according to expected utility. A second group of people may consistently and predictably choose not to treat. These individuals may be thought of as *action avoiders*. They choose not to make an active intervention when options are equal according to expected utility. Other individuals may choose treatment for one or two of the situations and no treatment for the other(s).

The three decisions ask about treatment at three different points in the natural history of SADS. The first situation asks about prevention before the disease develops (primary prevention), the second situation asks about prevention once there has been exposure (secondary prevention), and the third situation asks about prevention of complications once the disease has developed (tertiary prevention).

Even though the overall expected utility of each pair of options are equal, the probability of death in the absence of treatment in these three situations is quite different. The probabilities of death in the absence of treatment in these three situations are:

Situation A: primary prevention = .004 = 0.4%
Situation B: secondary prevention = .04 = 4%
Situation C: tertiary prevention = .1 = 10%

Thus the probability of death is 25 times as large (.004 versus .1) when the individual already has SADS compared with the individual who has not been exposed. When the probability of death is large, such as after SADS develops, far fewer individuals need to be treated to prevent one death. In addition, when treating SADS you are treating an *identifiable victim* (i.e., you and they know that they have a high probability of dying).

In contrast, when treating after exposure, a much larger number of individuals must be treated to prevent one death. In addition, the individuals who benefit have been called *statistical*

FIGURE 4-3

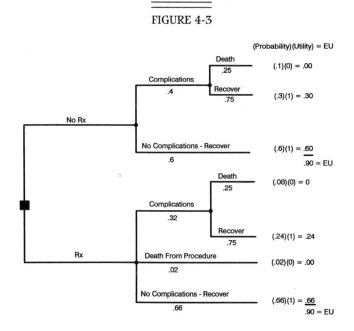

*beneficiaries*. Neither the clinician nor the patients knows who did not develop SADS due to the treatment and who would not have developed SADS even in the absence of treatment.

The situation is even worse for those who choose to treat prior to exposure. Even larger numbers of individuals need to be treated for each death that is prevented, and again those who benefit cannot be identified. In addition, those who have not even been exposed to SADS will still be exposed to the side effects of treatment. These individuals may develop side effects that are directly attributable to the treatment. Identifiable victims may blame a clinician; statistical beneficiaries don't say thank you. Thus, many clinicians may be inclined not to treat prior to exposure even if they are inclined to treat after SADS develops.

There are also some clinicians who select to treat prior to the development of disease but not after disease develops. What might motivate these individuals? These clinicians may be focusing on the fact that treatment prevents a higher proportion (50%) of cases of SADS when used prior to exposure (i.e. 4% versus 2%) compared to its ability to prevent complications after SADS has developed (40% versus 32%). These people may feel that developing SADS should be avoided even if there is eventual recovery. For them developing and recovering from SADS is worse than never developing SADS at all.

Thus, there are several patterns of choice. However, according to the expected utility principle there is no correct answer. When expected utilities are equal then other factors which distinguish between choices take on additional importance. We call the first of these factors that we have just illustrated *action inclination*.

The action inclination implies that considering the outcomes of our choices is not enough, we also need to consider the process that needs to occur. For those who consistently prefer action the dictum: don't just stand there do something may summarize their view of the process. The bias toward action can be very strong in cultures with a strong belief in the ability to successfully intervene in the disease process. When decisions are made using expected utilities without taking into account what needs to be done to implement the decision we are making the additional assumption that our action inclination does not affect our decisions.

Decision-makers may also disagree with the recommendation of a decision analysis because they disagree with the probabilities or utilities that have been included. Decision-makers often believe, correctly or incorrectly, that it is possible to estimate probabilities of outcomes for individual patients more accurately than using the probabilities based on the average patient, as is usually done in decision analysis. Clinicians confronted with SADS may believe that they can predict who will recover, who will respond to a particular therapy, or who will suffer the side effects. To the extent that individual prognosis can be predicted using measurable factors, it is possible to include these factors in the decision tree. Prognosis may also be predicted on the basis of an individual's course over a period of time, an individual's past response to treatment, or their rate of declining function. At times, each of these factors may be a very reliable gauge of the future course of a disease. In these situations, the probabilities estimated by the decision-maker should be used in the decision tree.[1]

Studies of decision-making have found that decision-makers may disagree with the recommendations of decision analysis even if they agree with all the probabilities and utilities which have been used in constructing the decision tree. Perhaps this is because our decisions do not really aim to maximize expected utility. Perhaps decision-makers are using a different decision principle. Thus, we will now take a look at other decision principles besides maximizing expected utility that are used in making treatment decisions. This will allow us to identify the particular decision principle which you prefer.

Even if a decision-maker wishes to use the maximize expected utility principle, the quantitative aspects of calculating expected utility are difficult to use. Even if all the probabilities and utilities were readily available a computer or at least a calculator is often needed to make decisions based on expected utilities. The approach to decision-making implied by expected utility theory does not reflect the approach most people actually use in making everyday decisions. Most of us cannot and do not make complicated calculations in our heads. In fact much of what we

---

[1] Another reason that individuals frequently deviate from the recommendations resulting from the maximizing expected utility principle is that this method is designed to determine which option produces the greater net benefit on average. However, individuals confronted with a decision may not care about what happens on average; they may care about what is most likely to happen to them. An individual often cannot repeat their decision; many times, they have only one choice and will have only one outcome. This is one reason that decision-making for individuals may differ from decision-making designed for groups.

do in decision-making even when dealing with numbers can be viewed as simplifying situations to avoid contending with complicated calculations or attempting to handle too much information at once.

Studies of decision-making have produced a series of important concepts about how medical decisions are actually made. These concepts help us understand why maximizing expected utility may not be the decision principle we actually use in making medical decisions.

> Concept 1: Both probabilities and utilities are treated as a very limited number of categories, not as continuous data from 0 to 1.

Studies of medical decision-making suggest that we think in categories, not in probabilities. Most people can deal with no more than 5 potential categories. Thus, we often translate numbers into categories or think directly in categories rather than thinking in numbers. For instance, one way to translate words into numbers is to use the following translation: very high probability > 95%; high probability 70–95%; moderate probability 30–70%; low probability 5–30%; and very low probability < 5%.

The scale used to score utilities in decision analysis also extends from 0 to 1 with an unlimited number of categories in between. Most likely we do not think of utilities as numbers; rather, we use categories. For instance, a patient with a current impairment of their health may use the following categories: (1) full, desired or perfect health; (2) improved acceptable health with limitations; (3) the current state of impaired health; (4) further impairment of health; (5) death.

> Concept 2: We do not think quantitatively about differences or changes in probabilities or in utilities, especially at the extremes of the scales.

Studies suggest that we have great difficulty dealing accurately with very low or very high probabilities. When an event such as a side effect is rare, for instance, less than 1%, individuals tend to either underestimate or overestimate its probability of occurrence. We may overestimate its probability and place it in the very low probability category, for instance less than 5%. Alternatively, we may regard it as very unlikely and thus ignore it effectively treating the probability of occurrence as zero. Thus within the most extreme category may be a range of probabilities from 0 to 5%.

The same basic problem occurs with utilities, especially at the low end of the scale. For instance, the difference between .8 and .9 is the same as the distance between .1 and 0. However, at the lower range of utility scores the differences in scores have very different implications. Zero is the irreversible state of death. What does .1 mean? Is it a state of permanent coma? Is it a more desirable way to die? Is it an intolerable state which holds a small hope of recovery?

Therefore, when dealing with utilities we need to realize that death is different. Thus, it may be especially difficult to combine the utilities for outcomes that produce death with those that produce forms of disability.[2]

Concept 3: We can only incorporate a limited amount of information at one time; thus, we prefer to compare only two options at a time.

Because individuals have great difficulty handling large amounts of data at one time, the methods used to make decisions often need to be simplified. Studies of decision-making suggest that when we are making decisions about whether or not to treat individuals we often proceed using the following approach:

1. First we identify a limited number of options for serious consideration.
2. Next we assess these options utilizing categories rather than numbers for probabilities and utilities.
3. Then we compare two options at a time making an overall assessment of which one is better.

Decision-making using this approach is similar to the way the optician assists a patient in selecting the best correction for eyeglasses. Individuals would have a great deal of difficulty if they were faced with a large number of choices and were required to merely go down the line assessing each correction. In selecting a lens we first narrow the choices by selecting a modest number of lenses for further consideration. Next we compare a pair of potential options. The best one is then compared to another option until

---

[2] *The Measures of Medicine* computer exercises illustrate and expand on the influence of the possibility of death on risk-taking tendencies.

it is rejected, or continues to be accepted compared one at a time to all the potentially viable options. Finally, the initial choice is confirmed by comparing it again to the potential alternatives. If the results are inconsistent, the process is repeated.

When comparing treatment options, individuals often try to determine which one does the better job of achieving the most important goal while doing a tolerable job of achieving other goals. This process occurs so automatically and unconsciously that we may not even recognize the principles which underlie our decisions. Thus, when making most decisions individuals do not calculate expected utility; rather decision principles are used that incorporate our preferences for seeking benefits and avoiding harms.[3]

Let us examine how this process of making decisions works by returning to an exercise using SADS.

---

■■Imagine that SADS and its treatment has resulted in a permanent disability that has left you with a quality of your health of .5 (remember 1 implies full health and 0 implies death on the utility scale).

Now imagine that there are two options from which you may choose one. The results of these options may produce no benefit and/or no harm or alternatively may:

- Produce a *full benefit* which raises the quality of your health by .4 points on the utility scale in which 1 = full health and 0 = death.
- Produce a *substantial benefit* which raises the quality of your health by .2 points on the utility scale in which 1 = full health and 0 = death.
- Produce a *substantial harm* which reduces the quality of your health by .2 points on the utility scale in which 1 = full health and 0 = death.

---

[3] When using this approach individuals are actually utilizing a decision-making approach by the rules rather than by the numbers. As is the case here, the use of rules rather than numbers is often easier to implement. In addition, choices are more predictable. That is, knowing the rule an individual favors we can often predict what they will decide in a particular situation. When using rules there are far fewer close calls compared to the use of quantitative techniques. All these factors may contribute to making decision-making by the rules rather than by the numbers more attractive to many decision-makers.

Which one of the two options (#1 or #2) do you prefer?

(For each option the potential benefits and also the potential harms are listed.)

Option #1:

| | | | |
|---|---|---|---|
| Full Benefit | — | 40% | No harm 90% |
| Substantial Benefit | — | 20% | and Substantial harm 10% |
| No Benefit | — | 40% | |

Option #2:

| | | | |
|---|---|---|---|
| Full Benefits | — | 0% | No harm 95% |
| Substantial Benefit | — | 95% | and Substantial harm 5% |
| No Benefit | — | 5% | |

Now let us take a look at another pair of options.

Which one of the two options (#2 or #3) do you prefer?

Option #2:

| | | | |
|---|---|---|---|
| Full Benefits | — | 0% | No harm 95% |
| Substantial Benefit | — | 95% | and Substantial harm 5% |
| No Benefiti | — | 5% | |

Option #3:

| | | | |
|---|---|---|---|
| Full Benefit | — | 20% | No harm 99% |
| Substantial Benefit | — | 51% | and Substantial harm 1% |
| No Benefit | — | 29% | |

These are complex decisions requiring complicated decision trees to display the potential outcomes. Despite the complicated nature of the decision trees most individuals can make this type of decision in their head. In making these decisions one of three different decision principles that correspond with the different options may have been used: (1) maximize full benefit (option #1); (2) maximize substantial benefit (option #2); or (3) minimize harm (option #3).

The first pair of options involves choosing between maximizing full benefit and maximizing substantial benefit. The second pair of options involves choosing between maximizing substantial benefit and minimizing harm. Depending on the choices made in these two pairs of options, your order of preference between the three options can be determined.

For instance, if you chose option #2 in the first pair and option #3 in the second pair, then your preference when overall expected utilities are equal is: minimizing harm is better than maximizing substantial benefit, which is better than maximizing full benefit.

Decision-making using this approach allows us to combine considerations of harms and benefits to make an overall assessment of the worth of an option. We can then compare the two options side-by-side. In performing this comparison we are revealing the principles that we use in making decisions. We will call this approach to decision making the *side-by-side approach,* since we are examining all the aspects of two options at one time.

This example may not seem realistic yet we often have to choose between maximizing the chances of obtaining the best possible or most desired outcome versus maximizing the probability of obtaining improvement. One therapy may fully restore function 50% of the time, yet may have a lower probability of bringing about improvement, (i.e., meaning partial restoration of function). Those who prefer to maximize the chances of improvements are said to be *satisficing*. They sacrifice maximum benefit to maximize their chances of getting an adequate or acceptable improvement.

Individuals fall into one of three general types of decision-makers: *benefit maximizers, satisficers,* and *harm minimizers*. For choices with only two options, such as prescribe or not prescribe, knowing the decision principle most important to you helps predict how you will decide.

The side-by-side approach is a very useful approach in decision-making because it allows simplification of the situation and allows us to consider only two options at a time. However, when in reality there are really three or more options, the use of the side-by-side approach can have an inherent problems; it may not always produce a consistent set of priorities. For instance, there are some individuals who have the following set of decision principles: maximizing full benefit is preferred to maximizing substantial benefit, and maximizing substantial benefit is preferred to minimizing harm, however, minimizing harm is preferred to maximizing full benefit.

In the previous set of options these individuals would have selected option #1 (maximize full benefit) when confronted with option #1 and #2. They would have selected option #2 (maximize substantial benefit) when faced with a choice between option #2 and #3. However, if confronted with a choice between option #1 (maximize full benefit) and #3 (minimize harm) they would have selected option #3 (minimize harm).

This type of inconsistency has the potential to occur quite frequently in medical decisions. For instance, imagine a patient with the following set of preferences: surgery is better than medicine; medicine is better than observation; observation is better than surgery. These preferences may seem quite reasonable or at least believable to you. However, the problem with these preferences is that they can lead to different choices depending on the order of presentation of the options. In fact, using the patient's own preferences we can manipulate the presentation to produce a choice of surgery, medicine, or observation. This manipulation can be done as follows.

If we wanted to produce the choice of medicine then we would ask the questions in the following order. "Which do you prefer, observation or surgery? Answer: observation." "Now which do you prefer, medicine or observation? Answer: medicine." Thus, this patient would choose medicine.

In contrast, if we wanted to produce a choice of surgery we would ask the questions in the following order. "Which do you prefer, medicine or observation? Answer: medicine." "Now which do you prefer, surgery or medicine? Answer: surgery." Thus, this patient would choose surgery. We can also produce a choice of observation by asking about medicine versus surgery first, then asking about surgery versus observation.

This potential for inconsistency is a problem that is inherent in the side-by-side approach. Whenever it is used to make decisions it is necessary to go back and ask the questions in a different order to see if the same results occur. That is why the clinician who is helping the patient select the best eyeglasses goes back at the end and confirms whether the patient has made a consistent choice.[4]

The side-by-side approach is very attractive to most people

---

[4] Another reason for the inconsistency which decision-makers at times demonstrate may be the fact that information is lost by creating categories instead of using scales from 0 to 1. At other times the source of the inconsistencies may be found by examining deviations from expected utility.

because it allows them to look at all the aspects of one option and compare it to all aspects of a second option. Often, however, we wish to or are forced to consider more than two options at the same time. Considering more than two options at the same time can add a great deal of complexity to decision-making.

When it is necessary to decide between three or more options another approach to decision-making is often used which is called *elimination-by-aspect*. Elimination-by-aspect implies that when confronted with three or more options we focus on harms and benefits separately. Choices are made by eliminating one at a time less desirable options that do not fulfill our decision principles for potential harms or potential benefits. This process often allows us to continue to make our final decision comparing the last two remaining options.

Now let us return to our SADS epidemic and face the even more difficult job of deciding between three complex options at a time.

---

Imagine that SADS and its treatment has resulted in a permanent disability which has left you with a quality of your health of .6 (remember 1 implies full health and 0 implies death on our utility scale).

Now imagine that there are three options from which you may choose one. The results of these options may produce no benefit and/or no harm or alternatively may:

- Produce a full benefit which raises the quality of your health by .4 on the utility scale in which 1 = full health and 0 = death.
- Produce a substantial benefit which raised the quality of your health by .2 on the utility scale in which 1 = full health and 0 = death.
- Produce a substantial harm which reduces the quality of your health by .2 on the utility scale in which 1 = full health and 0 = death.

Which one of the following three options (#1, #2, or #3) do you prefer?

(For each option the potential benefits and also the potential harms are listed).

Option #1:
|                     |   |       |                          |
|---------------------|---|-------|--------------------------|
| Full Benefit        | — | 40%   | No harm 90%              |
| Substantial Benefit | — | 20%   | and Substantial harm 10% |
| No Benefit          | — | 40%   |                          |

Option #2:
|                     |   |       |                          |
|---------------------|---|-------|--------------------------|
| Full Benefit        | — | 0%    | No harm 95%              |
| Substantial Benefit | — | 95%   | and Substantial harm 5%  |
| No Benefit          | — | 5%    |                          |

Option #3:
|                     |   |       |                          |
|---------------------|---|-------|--------------------------|
| Full Benefit        | — | 20%   | No harm 99%              |
| Substantial Benefit | — | 51%   | and Substantial harm 1%  |
| No Benefit          | — | 29%   |                          |

Figure 4-4 displays the previous three choices for treatment of SADS. According to expected utilities these options are all a toss-up; their expected utilities are all equal. Most people, however, have a preference for one of the three options.

If your decision principle previously was maximize benefit you probably still selected option #1; however, you most likely got there using a different approach. Perhaps you began by looking at the benefits and eliminating option #2, because it did not provide any probability of achieving full benefit. Then perhaps you eliminated option #3 because it had a lower probability of maximizing the benefits. Then possibly you looked at the resulting harms to be sure they were tolerable in relation to the benefits. Unless the harms seemed clearly excessive relative to the benefits you probably selected option #1.

If your decision principle previously was satisfice or maximize substantial benefit, you probably still selected option #2. First you looked at the benefits and eliminated the other two options one at a time. Then you looked at the harms to be sure they were not clearly excessive relative to the benefits. Unless the harm seemed clearly excessive relative to the benefits you selected option #2.

If your decision principle previously was minimize harm you probably still selected option #3. In contrast to the other two approaches you probably started by looking at the harms. In doing this you eliminated options #1 and then #2. Then

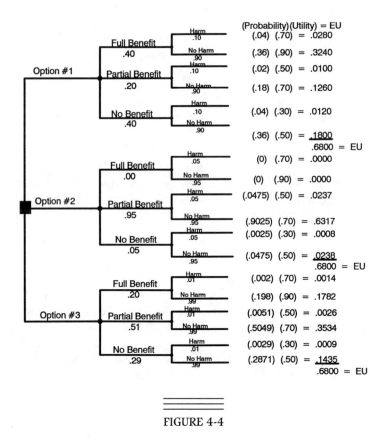

FIGURE 4-4

perhaps you looked at the benefits to be sure they were not so much greater that they outweighed the harms. Unless the benefits were far greater than the harms you probably selected option #3.

Using either the side-by-side approach or the elimination-by-aspect approach you most likely selected the same option. All three of these are common choices without an overwhelming preference among groups of medical students and health professionals.

By using the elimination-by-aspect approach, a complex situation involving three options can be dealt with. During most of the process, options can still be compared two at a time. The elimination-by-aspect approach allows a single choice between the three options and prevents the possibility of inconsistency.

The side-by-side and elimination-by-aspect approaches are qualitative approaches that have several important advantages.

- They allow us to think in categories rather than with numbers. Both probabilities and utilities are converted to categories. Thus despite all the numbers we are able to function without calculations.
- They allow us to compare two option at a time. Even in the elimination-by-aspect approach, we broke the choices down so that we were comparing our initial preference to one other option at a time.
- They permit us to avoid putting numbers on our choices. We need to state which option in each choice we preferred, but we do not need to state how much better it is.
- The decision rules we use lead to far fewer close choices or toss-ups than the expected utility approach. Despite the fact that many of these decisions were toss-ups according to expected utility calculations you probably had consistent preferences. In general, qualitative decision-making does not result in changes in the option chosen based on small changes in probabilities or utilities. Thus, the choices are generally more stable and predictable.

Thus, most of the time these approaches work very well. In fact most of our treatment decisions have traditionally been made using these approaches. Drugs and surgical procedures are usually thought of as having indications and contraindications. These categories conform with our desire to make qualitative decisions using "either-or" categories. First we determine whether or not a drug is indicated; then, if it is indicated, we make sure there is not a contraindication.

In more complex situations, such as those involving three or more options for treatment, we also incorporate the concepts of treatment of choice and relative contraindication. When a treatment of choice exists it provides a starting point for decision-making. Our decision-making tasks can then be limited to identifying a treatment of choice and determining whether a contraindication or relative contraindication is present. That is, after establishing the treatment of choice as the decision rule we look for exceptions to the rule. If a contraindication exists, then the option is eliminated and a secondary treatment is considered. Therefore, comparisons between treatments are only necessary when relative contraindications exist. Only then are we forced directly to balance benefits and harms. Most of the time we are able to side step this difficult reality.

Despite the many strengths of qualitative decision-making it has some inherent weaknesses. Many of these weakness are in exactly the areas where quantitative methods are most useful. The number of options for treatment and their potential outcomes are increasing rapidly as new treatments and new means of handling the complications of old treatments appear. Our ability to make active comparisons between several options at once is very limited because it requires manipulation of large amounts of information. When we feel ourselves overwhelmed by the number of options and all their potential outcomes, the structure of decision trees is especially helpful.

Often, the structure of decision analysis can help us think through the problem, allow us to consider the full range of options, and be sure we have considered all the potentially important outcomes. By considering all the options and all the potential outcomes, the decision trees may themselves be more complex than is necessary. A number of the potential outcomes may be rare enough to eliminate or may be combined with other similar outcomes. This conscious process called *pruning back* the decision tree allows systematic simplification of the decision-making process.

The categories used in qualitative decision-making at times can conceal more than they reveal. Two experts can disagree and make very different recommendations; yet, it may not be at all clear why they differ. The structure of decision analysis and sometimes the numbers used provide an essential framework for identifying the sources of differences of opinion. Decision-makers, including experts, may disagree concerning utilities, or probabilities, or because of the direction in which they deviate from the recommendations of expected utility. Thus, identifying the source of disagreement is an important use of decision analysis.

As we discussed, it is very difficult for most people to accurately assess very small probabilities. Small probabilities cannot be dealt with accurately in our heads. Rare side effects and rare complications, however, are an important part of medical decision-making. When multiple rare events are an important part of making a decision, quantitative methods such as decision analysis may be especially useful.

When there is a very low probability of success, quantitative methods may provide an objective basis for asking whether a treatment should be labeled as futile. The designation of futility implies that clinicians are not obligated to offer an available option even if individual patients might choose to receive the treatment. In fact, an increasingly important use of decision analysis is to help set practice policies or clinical guidelines for practice. These guidelines increasingly emphasize which treatments should be offered to patients as well as which treatments should not be offered.

The approaches examined thus far all share one aspect: they all aim to identify options in which the benefit to the decision-maker is greater than the harm. The decision-maker is usually one patient and the benefits and harms are usually viewed with respect to one patient. We have called this general approach to decision making *harm-benefit analysis,* whether it is performed quantitatively using decision trees and expected utilities or whether it is performed qualitatively.

Harm-benefit analysis implies that we aim to select options in which the benefits are greater than the harms, even if this is not always performed perfectly. Expected utility theory explicitly tells us to select the option in which the benefit exceeds the harm even if the additional benefit is very small. Thus individual decision-makers are advised to select options that provide them with a small increase in net benefit without ever recognizing the overall impact of many similar decisions.

What is the cumulative impact of a large number of individual decisions each of which has a slightly greater benefit than harm as viewed by an individual decision-maker? Often the most important impact of all these cumulative decisions is to greatly increase financial costs without substantially increasing the net health benefit.

This process cannot continue indefinitely. There is a limit to the percentage of a society's resources that can be devoted to health services. Thus there is a point at which the financial costs of decisions must also be considered. In Part II of *The Measures of*

*Medicine* we will take a look at one way that we can include considerations of cost.[5]

Before you go on, however, you might want to step back and review the issues that have been presented so far. The appendix at the end of the book summarizes the steps that we take in performing a harm-benefit decision analysis using a decision tree. The assumptions which we make are also outlined. In addition, you are now ready to take a look at Part I of *The Measures of Medicine* computer exercises which are included with the book. Part I will ask you to define your own utilities and use them to examine your own risk-taking attitudes.

[5] Costs have not been considered as part of harm-benefit analysis. It is possible to consider financial costs as a harm and thus incorporate costs into harm-benefit analysis. Alternatively it is possible to perform a harm-benefit analysis without considering financial costs. The results of a harm-benefit analysis are then really recommendations that need to be considered in light of cost consideration. The consideration of costs which follow in Part II assume that costs will only be directly considered at the social, community, or population level. This is really an oversimplification, since cost considerations can also have major impacts on individual decision-making.

# PART

# II

## Benefits, Harms, and Costs

# CHAPTER FIVE

## Cost-Effectiveness

It is now 2005 and your community of Simplicity has become a metropolitan area of 1,000,000 people. In Simplicity it was recognized over a decade ago that expenditures for health services had been increasing faster than any other expenditure.

During the years of dramatically increasing costs, the health system in Simplicity did not take costs into consideration. It wasn't like buying a car where the consumer considers the benefits (like performance), the harms (like safety), and also considers the costs. Rather, individuals who had insurance coverage generally received all services for which they or their physicians felt the benefits exceeded the harms.

There was no overall level of expenditures or cap placed on how much money Simplicity could spend on health. Thus it was not surprising that the expenditures rose every year until they hit almost 15% of the goods and services produced in Simplicity, the gross domestic product.

By then the cost of care had become a burden to the average family. Yet, the inadequacy of insurance coverage had kept many from receiving even highly effective preventive and curative services. Constantly increasing insurance payments were eating deeply into the raises that employers could afford, in effect lowering the standard of living. Something had to be done.

To deal with this crisis the citizens of Simplicity recognized that costs had to be considered. They approved a system based on the following basic principles:

1. Everyone is covered for effective basic preventive services based on a yearly fixed budget.
2. Cost-effective health services are covered as part of a package of services which everyone must obtain through a combination of individual payment, employer payment, and government support.
3. Additional health services, above and beyond those covered in the package, may be purchased by individuals out-of-pocket when they receive the services, or through purchase of additional insurance.

Having agreed upon these fundamental principles for the health care system in Simplicity, the job had just begun. It was necessary to develop a set of operating principles which would help make choices to determine exactly what was covered by each of these basic principles. Specifically, they needed to answer the following three questions:

- How can we make choices which maximize effectiveness when we have more than one effective preventive intervention and a yearly budget within which we must live?
- How can we determine which package of health services will allow us to maximize effectiveness while minimizing costs?
- How can we recognize when health services that are effective do not produce enough additional benefit to be worth the additional cost?

To put into effect what came to be called the cost-effectiveness system, the citizens of Simplicity built upon what they had learned when dealing with harms and benefits. In addition they adopted some economic principles which helped them build their new cost-effective health care system.

Because of your understanding of benefits and harms, you have recently been appointed Head of Health for Simplicity. It is your job to help the citizens of Simplicity reach a consensus on what should be covered in their system. You make recommendations to the community just like you previously made recommendations to individual patients.

Even before accepting this new position you recognize that you will need to look at the world quite a bit differently. Now you will need to consider the costs of services not just their benefits and harms. In addition, you will need to take a social or population perspective looking out for the community as a whole and not just your individual patient.

It is not long before you are faced with your first challenge in your new job. This decision will require you to deal with how to implement the first basic principle—that is, how to choose between effective preventive services when you have only a fixed yearly budget.

---

In Simplicity there are two preventable diseases called Paralysis and Coronary which affect people who have previously been in full health. During the next year 0.5% of the population of Simplicity will develop Paralysis and 1% of the population will develop Coronary.

Those who develop Paralysis, on average, will be left permanently with a quality of their health of .50. Those who develop Coronary, on average, will be left permanently with a quality of their health of .40.

There are new preventive methods available for both Paralysis and Coronary. Each treatment provides complete protection without any side effects. The prevention of one case of Paralysis costs $200,000 and the prevention of one case of Coronary costs $100,000.

Unfortunately, all is not so simple in Simplicity, even under the new system. This year there is an average of $1,000 per person to spend on new prevention efforts. There is no other way to obtain prevention. Thus you have enough money to prevent all cases of Paralysis, or all cases of Coronary, or you can choose to prevent neither.

You must make a recommendation to the citizens of Simplicity on how they should spend an average of $1,000 per person this year, or a total of $1,000,000,000.

---

**WILL YOU RECOMMEND PAYMENT FOR PREVENTION OF PARALYSIS, OF CORONARY, OR NEITHER?**

Thus far, we have used decision anyalysis to examine the way benefits and harms are assessed when making decisions for or by individuals. We have acted as if optimal decision-making involves selecting the alternative in which the health benefits exceed, to the greatest extent, the harms to health. We have called this approach maximizing expected utility.

Consideration of costs naturally comes after considerations of effectiveness. There is no reason to consider paying for a treatment if it does not have net benefit or effectiveness (i.e., if the benefits are not greater than the harms). Thus, we do not need to start over; we can build upon the techniques we have learned.

Once we pay attention to costs, however, we will not always choose the alternative that yields the greatest net benefit. Instead, we may choose an option that is less effective but far less expensive.

We can start by looking at a decision tree which presents the potential outcomes of each of our choices. Figure 5–1 displays the outcomes which result from choosing to prevent Paralysis, Coronary, and no prevention. Notice that both prevention of Paralysis and prevention of Coronary have an expected utility that is larger than the no prevention option. Thus, both prevention of paralysis and prevention of coronary have a net benefit compared to no prevention.

Also notice that the decision tree tells us that preventing Coronary has greater effectiveness than preventing Paralysis. This is the case because there is a greater probability of Coronary—and prevention of Coronary results, on average, in a greater gain in utility.

When effectiveness has been demonstrated, as it has been for prevention of Paralysis and Coronary, we can then look at the costs. Unfortunately, you are in the position of having to choose between two treatments that have both been shown to have effectiveness. Because of the financial constraints you can recommend coverage of prevention for Paralysis or prevention of Coronary, but not both.

Cost-effectiveness is a method for helping us make choices between alternatives when resources are limited and our goal is to use those resources to maximize the overall health benefit, while minimizing the cost to the community. In maximizing the overall health benefit to the community we will not maximize the benefit to each and every individual in the community. In fact, whenever we choose to cover some services that have been shown to have effectiveness and not to cover others, there is an

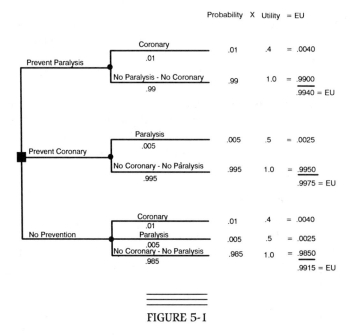

FIGURE 5-1

inherent conflict between what is best for the community and what is best for those individuals whose services are not covered.

If either prevention of Paralysis or prevention of Coronary is not covered, there will be individuals who could have had a better outcome. Thus, now our goal is not just to maximize effectiveness, but to maximize effectiveness, given that we are constrained by cost (i.e., our fixed yearly budget of $1,000,000,000 for new preventive services).

Let us begin our examination of cost-effectiveness by calculating how much effectiveness we can provide if we spend all the budget on prevention of Coronary, and alternatively, how much effectiveness we can provide if we spend the entire budget on prevention of Paralysis.

First we have to be sure of what we mean by effectiveness. Effectiveness is really the same concept we looked at when we examined benefits and harms. It is the benefits minus the harms, or the net benefit. There is one difference, however; now we are always interested in the benefits and the harms that occur not only to the individuals who receive treatment, but to other individuals in the society as well. This would be important, for instance, if one condition was an infectious disease, or had consequences for the next generation.

So far when we measured effectiveness we used as a unit of measurement the quality-adjusted lives saved. We can start by using quality-adjusted lives saved here as well. When comparing two alternatives, either of which will use up our entire budget, we can calculate what is called a *cost-effectiveness ratio*. The cost-effectiveness (C/E) ratio is defined as follows:

$$\text{Cost-effectiveness (C/E) ratio} = \frac{\text{Cost}}{\text{Effectiveness}}$$

Notice that the C/E ratio tells us the cost relative to the effectiveness. That is, it tells us how much we need to pay on average to obtain one unit of effectiveness. The unit of effectiveness we have used up to now is one life at full health, or a quality-adjusted life.

To calculate a C/E ratio for Paralysis and also for Coronary we need to know the costs of preventing each condition and the effectiveness of the prevention measured in our units of measurement (i.e., in quality-adjusted lives).

Let us start by calculating the effectiveness of preventing paralysis and the effectiveness of preventing coronary. When dealing with groups of individuals rather than one individual we can think of effectiveness as the multiplication product as follows:

$$\text{Effectiveness} = \begin{array}{l}\text{(\# of cases of disease prevented)} \times \text{(average} \\ \text{utility gained from prevention of the disease)}\end{array}$$

The number of cases of the disease prevented can be calculated by multiplying the following:

$$\begin{array}{l}\text{\# of cases of the} \\ \text{disease prevented}\end{array} = \begin{array}{l}\text{(Probability of developing the disease)} \times \\ \text{(\# of individuals in Simplicity)}\end{array}$$

Thus to calculate effectiveness we multiply the following[1]:

$$\text{Effectiveness} = \begin{array}{c}\text{(Probability of developing the disease)} \times \\ \text{(\# of individuals in Simplicity)} \times \\ \text{(average utility gained)}\end{array}$$

---

[1] Notice that this formula includes the probability times the utility and is thus really the expected utility times the number of individuals in Simplicity.

Let us use this formula to calculate effectiveness for Paralysis and for Coronary:

For Paralysis:

$$\text{Effectiveness} = (.005)(1,000,000)(1 - .5)$$
$$= 2,500 \text{ quality-adjusted lives saved}$$

Thus, 2,500 quality-adjusted lives saved result from preventing 5,000 cases of Paralysis (i.e., 0.5% of 1,000,000). Each of these cases on average yields a quality of life improvement of .5 (i.e., $1 - .5$).

For Coronary:

$$\text{Effectiveness} = (.01)(1,000,000)(1 - .4)$$
$$= 6,000 \text{ quality-adjusted lives saved}$$

Thus, 6,000 quality-adjusted lives saved result from preventing 10,000 cases of Coronary (i.e., 1% of 1,000,000). Each of these cases, on average, yields a quantity of life improvement of .6 (i.e., $1 - .4$). (Remember, we are assuming that the previous health status of those who would develop both Paralysis and Coronary is full health with a utility of 1).

Now let us look at the costs of preventing Paralysis and of preventing Coronary. The total costs of prevention are:

$$\frac{\text{Cost of}}{\text{prevention}} = \frac{(\text{\# of cases of the disease prevented}) \times}{(\text{average cost of preventing a case of the disease})}$$

Thus, to calculate costs we perform the following calculations:

$$\frac{\text{Cost of}}{\text{prevention}} = \frac{(\text{Probability of developing the disease}) \times}{(\text{\# of individuals in Simplicity}) \times}{(\text{average cost of preventing a case of the disease})}$$

Let us use this formula to calculate cost for prevention of Paralysis and also for Coronary:

$$\text{Cost of Prevention of Paralysis} = (.005)\,(1,000,000)\,(\$200,000)$$
$$= \$1,000,000,000$$

$$\text{Cost of Prevention of Coronary} = (.01)\,(1,000,000)\,(\$100,000)$$
$$= \$1,000,000,000$$

Thus prevention of Paralysis and prevention of Coronary each cost $1,000,000,000. This just happens to be the total amount you have in your budget. Thus, as already suspected, Simplicity's current prevention budget for new preventive treatment is just enough to cover prevention of Paralysis, or prevention of Coronary—but not both.

Now we can calculate the C/E ratio for Paralysis and also for Coronary.

$$\text{C/E ratio} = \frac{\text{Cost}}{\text{Effectiveness}}$$

$$\text{C/E Paralysis} = \frac{\$1,000,000,000}{2,500 \text{ Quality-adjusted lives saved}}$$

$$= \frac{\$400,000}{\text{Quality-adjusted life saved}}$$

$$\text{C/E Coronary} = \frac{\$1,000,000,000}{6,000 \text{ Quality-adjusted lives saved}}$$

$$= \frac{\$166,666}{\text{Quality-adjusted life saved}}$$

Prevention of Coronary costs \$166,666 per quality-adjusted life saved, and prevention of Paralysis costs \$400,000 per quality-adjusted life saved. Thus, the cost-effectiveness ratio suggests that if you must choose between prevention of Paralysis and prevention of Coronary, prevention of Coronary leads to a lower cost per quality-adjusted life saved.

Thus, you might argue that prevention of Coronary is the better choice. However, remember that now we are making recommendations for the community, not just for individuals one at a time. From the perspective of the community we may want to know how long the individuals whose disease is prevented are expected to live. That is, we may need to consider not only how many lives will be saved, but how many years of life are saved. Thus, from the health as well as the economic point of view, we might want to take into account the length of life, or number of years of life saved. It is possible to take into account the number of years of life saved using a measurement known as *life-expectancy*.

The age of those who develop a disease is important because

in general the younger the individuals the longer they still have
to live. If we are interested in the number of years of life saved
and not just the number of lives saved we need to take into
account the age of the individuals.

> ■■Paralysis is a disease that occurs in children with an average
> age of 14; Coronary is a disease that occurs in adults with an
> average age of 60.                                              ■■

### HOW DOES THE AGE OF THOSE AFFECTED INFLUENCE YOUR DECISION?

To incorporate the consideration of age into a cost-effectiveness
analysis, we must estimate what is called the *life-expectancy*. To
estimate life-expectancy we need to know how many individuals
die each year in Simplicity and their age at death. This can be
obtained from the death certificates in Simplicity. We also need
data on the number of individuals alive at each age at the beginning of a year. This can be obtained based on a census of the
population. Knowing the number of individuals who die and the
number who are alive at the beginning of the year 2005, for
instance, it is possible to calculate the probability of death for
each age group as follows:

$$\text{Probability of death in one age group in 2005} = \frac{\text{Number of deaths in 2005 in the age group}}{\text{Number of individuals alive at the beginning of 2005 in the same age group}}$$

Once we have obtained the probability of death in each
age group in 2005, we can envision an imaginary person who
is born and lives out their entire life span faced with the
probabilities of death of the citizens of Simplicity in 2005.
That is, in 2005 this imaginary person has the probability of
death of 0 to 1 year olds; in 2006 they have the probability of
death of 1 to 2 year olds in 2005 in Simplicity; in 2007 they
have the probability of death of 2 to 3 year olds in 2005 in
Simplicity. Using these probabilities from each age group it is

possible to obtain the average life-expectancy for this imaginary individual.[2]

This life-expectancy is called the *life-expectancy at birth* since it uses all the probabilities of death beginning with the first year of life. For a 14 year old, life-expectancy is calculated using all the probabilities of death beyond age 14 in 2005, while for a 60 year old, life-expectancy is calculated using all the probabilities of death beyond age 60 in 2005.

In Simplicity in the year 2005 the life-expectancy for individuals who have reached the age of 14 is 66 years. That is, a 14 year old is expected to live, on average, to 80 years. For those who have reached the age of 60 their life-expectancy is 22 years. They are expected, on average, to live to the age of 82.[3]

Thus, it is possible to estimate the average years of remaining life or the life-expectancy for individuals of different ages if we are willing to assume that data on the probability of death will remain the same in future years. In other words, our ability to predict average length of life in the future assumes that nothing will change, (i.e., the probabilities of death among each age group will neither go higher nor lower). Thus we cannot realistically expect our life-expectancies to predict how long either particular individuals or groups of people will live. Nonetheless, calculation of life-expectancy is the best measure we have for comparing the probability of death in the future, and for comparing one group or population to another.[4]

---

[2] Life-expectancy is actually calculated by introducing the concept of a *stationary population* in which the same number of individuals are born into the population each year evenly throughout the year. In this stationary population there is no immigration or migration. Thus, in this population the number of persons alive in any one age group will never change. In this stationary population it is then possible to calculate the average number of years of life that remains upon reaching a particular age. This average number of remaining years is the expectation of life or life-expectancy.

[3] The life-expectancy at age 60 is 2 years more than the difference between 60 and 14. In other words once you have made it to age 60 your life-expectancy estimates your average age of death as 82, rather than 80. Having reached age 60, you would have survived though age intervals where some individuals have died.

[4] The life-expectancy discussed here assumes that the individual or group we are interested in has the same life-expectancy as the rest of the members of their age group in the population. However, with medical or public health decisions we often deal with individuals or groups with a known disease. Their probabilities of death may be much greater than those of the average person. Probabilities that reflect the known probabilities of death from a par-

Now let us see what happens when we incorporate life-expectancy into our decision whether to prevent Paralysis or alternatively to prevent Coronary.

Remember that by preventing Coronary we could save 6,000 quality-adjusted lives. By preventing Paralysis we could save 2,500 quality-adjusted lives. On average the lives saved by preventing Coronary have a life-expectancy of 22 years, compared with 66 years for those lives saved by preventing Paralysis. Thus we can multiply the number of quality-adjusted lives saved by the life-expectancy to obtain a measurement called the *quality-adjusted life years* or often known as *QALYs*. The number of QALYs is calculated as follows:

$$\#\,\text{of QALYs} = \frac{(\#\text{ of quality-adjusted lives saved}) \times}{(\text{average life-expectancy of the lives saved})}$$

QALYs are the basic unit used in cost-effectiveness analysis. The term *cost-utility anyalysis* is increasingly being applied to the specific type of cost-effectiveness analysis in which the health outcome is measured in QALYs. QALYs are as vital to health economics as the measurement of vital signs in patient care. Unfortunately measuring QALYs is far less cut-and-dried than measuring patient vital signs.[5]

One QALY is equal to one year at full health for one individual. It can result from a gain of one year of full health for one individual who would have died otherwise. This is the situation because this one individual's quality of health would be equal to 1 instead of 0 on our utility scale. Alternatively, QALYs can

ticular disease can be incorporated into life-expectancy calculations. A simple approximation known as the Declining Exponential Approximation of Life-Expectancy (DEALE) is often used. The DEALE makes the assumption that life-expectancy is equal to one divided by the sum of an individual's demographically derived mortality rate (here limited to considerations of age), plus the mortality rate associated with their particular disease. More precise estimates can also be made.

[5] The term cost-effectiveness analysis is a generic term that applies to several types of analysis. It generally implies an economic analysis in which there is an assessment of a particular health outcome per monetary unit, such as dollars. However, the measurement of outcome may vary. When two or more options are being compared that all produce the same outcome (such as prevention of blindness), then the unit used may be one case of blindness. However, when the aim is to compare treatment for different diseases or treatments for the same disease that produces more than one potential outcome, a common unit of measurement is needed. Quality-adjusted life years (QALYs) serve this goal of providing a common unit of measurement.

result from adding together brief or partial improvements from more than one individual. More than one year of life lived at less than full health can also be added to produce one or more QALYs.

The total number of QALYs produced by any option is calculated by multiplying the number of quality-adjusted lives saved and the average life-expectancy of the lives saved. Thus for Coronary and Paralysis the total number of QALYs are:

$$\text{Paralysis} = (2,500)(66) = 165,000 \text{ QALYs}$$

$$\text{Coronary} = (6,000)(22) = 132,000 \text{ QALYs}$$

The life-expectancy for the average person in whom Paralysis would have developed is three times as long as the life-expectancy of the average person in whom Coronary would have developed. This difference in life-expectancy results in more QALYs for the prevention of Paralysis and thus greater effectiveness (as measured by QALYs) for the prevention of Paralysis than for the prevention of Coronary.

Now we can calculate the C/E ratio using cost per QALY instead of cost per quality-adjusted life saved. The cost-effectiveness ratios for Paralysis and Coronary are:

$$\text{C/E ratio Paralysis} = \frac{\$1,000,000,000}{165,000 \text{ QALY}} = \frac{\$6,061}{\text{QALY}}$$

$$\text{C/E ratio Coronary} = \frac{\$1,000,000,000}{132,000 \text{ QALYs}} = \frac{\$7,576}{\text{QALY}}$$

Now preventing Paralysis looks better than Coronary, at least in terms of how much it costs to provide a QALY. However, notice that the use of QALYs put those who are currently elderly at a disadvantage. Treating each year of life-expectancy the same makes it look more attractive to provide treatment for the young since we may be able to obtain more QALYs for each life saved.

It has been argued that the elderly are not really placed at a disadvantage overall if you consider the fact that they have made it to their current age at least in part because of the resources that were previously spent on the young. The age issue is an example of what has been called *distributional issues*. Distributional issues deal with which groups within society receive the benefits, which ones suffer the harms, and which ones bear the costs.[6]

Well, you are a bit uneasy with the implications for the elderly, but since that seems to be the way things are done under the health system in Simplicity you recommend spending the $1,000,000,000 for preventing Paralysis, and not for preventing Coronary. In doing this you are implementing the first basic principle of Simplicity's health system. You are making choices that maximize effectiveness when there is more than one effective preventive intervention and a yearly budget which constrains the amount we can spend.

The basic principles at work in Simplicity have forced us into a difficult choice. They have done this in part because we have not been able to compare the cost-effectiveness of preventing Paralysis or preventing Coronary to other alternatives for prevention or for cure. If we could compare the costs of preventing Paralysis or Coronary with other alternative uses of money we might want to spend enough money to prevent both diseases.

Thus at times prevention is placed at a disadvantage if treated as a separate category with a fixed yearly budget, rather than being compared to the cost-effectiveness of other health services. In Simplicity your only choice is to recommend an increase in next year's prevention budget to cover both prevention of Coronary and prevention of Paralysis.

In evaluating the costs of preventing Coronary and preventing Paralysis we have been presented with the costs, without knowing what the the costs are actually measuring. Thus we need to step back and take a look at what costs are measuring.

[6] The age issue is the only distributional issue that is directly addressed as part of cost-effectiveness analysis. However, there is also a built-in advantage to providing effective services to the healthy, compared to the disabled (i.e., those with permanent reductions in utility which are unaffected by the service). The advantage in providing services to the healthy occurs because disabled individuals have a reduced utility already. Thus, the potential QALYs gained are less for each additional year of life provided. Other issues of distribution between groups—such as between the rich and poor or advantaged and disadvantaged—are not generally incorporated into cost-effectiveness analyses, as will be discussed in chapter 9.

# CHAPTER SIX

## Costs: What are They Measuring?

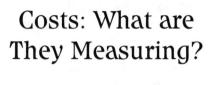

What is covered in the costs? This is a critical question that must be answered before implementing the basic principles of Simplicity's health system. Thus, before we go on to look at how we implement these principles we need to learn more about what we mean by costs. Let us examine the question of costs by turning to the next problem you face as Head of Health.

> Simplicity is considering paying for a new treatment called Pneumogone. Pneumogone has been shown to have a greater probability of cure for patients who have a common potentially fatal form of pneumonia than other available treatments. Pneumogone prevents recurrence of this type of pneumonia during the next year but not beyond the first year.
>
> However, Pneumogone is more expensive than other treatments. It costs more per administration and it requires patients to return for treatment after discharge from the hospital. Your next job as Head of Health for Simplicity is to estimate what the costs would be if you approve the use of Pneumogone.

Your first inclination in calculating costs is simply to ask the price of Pneumogone and how many doses are needed. However, it's not quite so simple. Actually, when health economists talk about cost they are really talking about what they call *opportunity costs*. Opportunity costs are the value of alternatives that could be achieved with the same resources. Thus economists are not really asking about prices unless prices are an accurate indication of the amount of resources required.[1]

Even if prices accurately reflect the resources required, the calculation of costs is not so straightforward. When economists talk about costs they do not limit their calculation to prices that must be paid to purchase and administer Pneumogone. They are really interested in all the current and future expenditures and savings of resources which results from the decision to administer Pneumogone. Furthermore, the terminology used when calculating costs can be very confusing. The terms *direct* and *indirect costs,* for instance, may be used in several very different ways.[2]

Because of the confusion that can occur due to the multiple use of the same terms by such professionals as accountants, economists, and health administrators, we will refer to the component of costs using descriptive expressions rather than technical terms. The categories of costs and cost savings used in cost-effectiveness analyses have at times included the following:

---

[1] Prices are often determined by negotiation and may be artificially set. Prices charged for health services are often increased or decreased to shift costs from one service or activity to another. This process is called *cost shifting*. When prices do not reflect resource costs, the results of a cost–effectiveness analysis will not make sense. The analysis will not reflect what we want it to reflect (i.e., social costs of the resources needed to provide the services). In a cost-effectiveness analysis benefits and harms should also be included from a social perspective, (i.e., they should be included regardless of who is affected and when they are affected).

[2] The terms *direct* and *indirect costs* may be used to distinguish the costs of providing services used by particular service programs, versus the cost of overhead or indirect costs that provide services needed by multiple programs. Alternatively the term *direct costs* may be used to indicate costs attributable to a disease, whereas *indirect cost* may be used to indicate costs that occur because of the additional years of life that result from treatment. For instance, indirect cost may refer to the cost of treating other diseases that affect individuals who survive because of the treatment. In addition, direct and indirect costs are often used to imply what we will call medical versus nonmedical costs.

1. Medical input costs (sometimes called direct costs): All the costs of producing the services; the costs induced by the need to treat side effects or harms from the treatment; and the cost savings from reduced complications or recurrences due to the treatment.

   Medical input costs can be divided into the following categories:

   - Production costs: The costs of delivering the services required to provide the potential benefit. For Pneumogone this cost might include the cost of the drug and the equipment for its administration, the personnel costs, as well as the overhead costs required to provide the service.
   - Induced costs: The costs of diagnosing and treating side effects of treatment.
   - Induced cost savings: Cost savings due to reduced disease complications. The cost savings of Pneumogone may be attributed to the reduction in hospitalization and other medical care costs due to a reduction in recurrent pneumonia or complications of the original illness.

2. Nonmedical input costs (sometimes called indirect costs): The costs of obtaining care and the lost income due to obtaining care, or from being disabled. These costs or savings can be divided into two categories:

   - Access costs (or cost savings): These costs include the extra patient time spent and expenses such as the transportation required to obtain the service (the Pneumogone), to obtain treatment for side effects, as well as the cost savings from not having to seek these services for complications or recurrences of pneumonia.
   - Disability costs (or cost savings): The cost of payments which need to be made because of illness are additional disability costs. Reductions in disability due to a more rapid return to work can be reduced from the costs of disability.

3. Medical costs of success: The additional cost of other medical services that must be provided for individuals who survive longer because they do not die from the original or

recurrent pneumonia. These costs include the cost of care for diseases currently present as well as the cost of diagnosing and treating new diseases.

4. Nonmedical costs of success: The additional costs of providing nonmedical services, including the costs of daily living such as food, clothing, and shelter for those who survive longer because of Pneumogone.

Now, fortunately, the well-developed data system in Simplicity can provide opportunity costs per person for providing coverage for Pneumogone as follows.

Medical input costs:
    Production costs = $300
    Induced costs (all in the following year) = $20
    Induced cost savings (all in the following year) = −$200
Nonmedical input costs:
    Access costs = $100
    Disability cost (cost savings) = −$175
Medical costs of success:
    One year after use of Pneumogone until age 65 = $50
    After age 65 = $150
Nonmedical costs of success:
    After age 65 = $250

Now you need to decide which of these costs to include. To illustrate the point, let us examine how costs are seen by different citizens and groups in Simplicity who look at the health care system from a variety of view points or perspectives.[3]

1. A health insurance company with a short-term (1 year) obligation to pay for services.
2. An employer with a responsibility to pay for all health services and disability until age 65.
3. A government health system with an obligation to pay for health services for an entire lifetime.
4. A government with an obligation to pay disability, health services for an entire lifetime, as well as social security to cover basic living expenses after age 65.

---

[3] All the perspectives discussed here are the perspectives of those who pay for care. As we will demonstrate in chapter 9, the perspectives of those who provide services may be very different. In general, cost-effectiveness analysis is most applicable to those who pay for care. However, as illustrated here, there are a number of different payer perspectives.

5. A patient who is entitled to the payments under the system in number 4.

FOR EACH OF THESE PERSPECTIVES, WHICH TYPES OF COSTS WOULD YOU WANT TO INCLUDE IN YOUR COST-EFFECTIVENESS ANALYSIS? WHAT ARE THE DOLLAR COSTS FROM EACH OF THESE PERSPECTIVES?

**1. Insurance company with short-term contract:**    Imagine that you are an executive in a fee-for-service insurance plan and are responsible for paying the costs for a large group. You are responsible for paying the costs of all health services utilized over a short period of time (i.e., one year). When considering whether to cover Pneumogone, what costs would you take into account?

You would be interested in the production costs because these costs will result in charges to your company. You would also be interested in the induced medical costs if the costs of treating side effects and cost savings from future care for pneumonia are likely to occur during the short-run period. Because you will not generally be responsible for the nonmedical costs of access or disability costs you would not generally be interested in including these costs. Likewise, because the medical and nonmedical costs of success occur in the longer-run future they may not be of importance to you, since your company would not necessarily be responsible for paying for these service. Thus, the costs of interest are:

| | |
|---|---|
| Production costs .................. | $300 |
| Induced costs ..................... | $ 20 |
| Induced cost savings ............... | −$200 |
| Total ........................... | $ 80 per use |

**2. Employer:**    As an employer responsible for all employee health services and disability costs for those under 65 you would be interested in several of these categories of costs. Because you are paying for health services you would be interested in the medical input costs including production and induced costs. In addition, you may be interested in the nonmedical costs including disability costs because you may have to pay the cost of disability. Because you remain responsible for your employees health services until age 65 you may be interested in the medical cost of success until age 65.[4]

---

[4] It is a simplification to say that a particular individual will totally ignore costs which do not have an immediate impact on their budget. An employer may be

Thus the costs of interest are:

| | |
|---|---:|
| Production costs .................... | $300 |
| Induced costs ..................... | $ 20 |
| Induced cost savings ............... | −$200 |
| Disability ........................ | −$175 |
| Medical cost of success < 65 ......... | $ 50 |
| Total ........................... | −$ 5 per use |

## 3. Government Health System with Long-Run Responsibility:

Imagine that you are responsible for the finance system for a national health insurance system that pays for the health care expenses for a segment of the population or the entire population. This may be a comprehensive national health system as it exists in many nations. What costs would be of interest to you?

As with the short-term insurance system, you would be interested in the medical production costs. You would also be interested in the induced costs and induced savings, even if they occurred a number of years in the future. Thus all the medical input costs would be of concern. The nonmedical costs, whether they are access costs or disability costs, would not be of importance to you because your system is only responsible for the health services expenses.

However, you might be interested in the medical costs of success. In fact these may be very large costs if an individual is kept alive for long periods and another disease develops that requires extensive medical care. If the patients who benefit from Pneumogone go on to develop other diseases which require expensive therapy either before or after age 65 you would want to include these costs as well. Thus the costs of interest are:

| | |
|---|---:|
| Production cost .................... | $300 |
| Induced costs ..................... | $ 20 |
| Induced costs savings .............. | −$200 |
| Medical costs of success <65 ........ | $ 50 |
| Medical costs of success >65 ........ | $150 |
| Total ........................... | $320 per use |

concerned about the out-of-pocket expenditures of their employees and a politician may be concerned about the costs that must be paid by voters.

**4. Government with disability and social security as well as health services responsibility:** A government that provides additional coverage beyond health services would be interested in all the costs discussed for the governmental health services as well as additional costs. Because the government is responsible for the costs of disability and for basic living expenses under a social security system the future costs of these expenses would also be of interest. Thus the costs of interest are:

| | |
|---|---:|
| Production cost .................... | $300 |
| Induced costs ..................... | $ 20 |
| Induced cost savings .............. | −$200 |
| Disability ........................ | −$175 |
| Medical costs of success <65 ........ | $ 50 |
| Medical costs of success >65 ........ | $150 |
| Nonmedical costs of success ........ | $250 |
| Total ............................ | $395 per use |

**5. Patient:** As a patient covered by the full government system you would only be interested in the costs that you have to pay out-of-pocket. Assuming that the $395 indicated previously is already covered, the only remaining costs are the costs of accessing the system. Thus the costs of interest are:

| | |
|---|---:|
| Access cost ....................... | $100 |
| Total ............................ | $100 per use |

Thus the costs can vary from −$5 per use from the perspective of the employer to + $395 from the perspective of the government with multiple program responsibilities. Now you realize it depends on how you look at costs. However, you still need an answer to the basic question:

WHICH COSTS SHOULD BE INCLUDED IN A COST-EFFECTIVENESS ANALYSIS?

Health economists have been arguing about what costs to include for years. However, there is now a general consensus. There are really two issues that need to be decided:

1. From what perspective should a cost-effectiveness analysis be done?
2. Which costs are legitimate to include once the perspective is chosen?

In theory a cost-effectiveness analysis can be done from any of the previously discussed perspectives and from others as well. For those who have a perspective that does not include all the costs such as a patient or an employer someone else is picking up the additional costs. Thus economists favor a perspective that includes all the legitimate costs related to the treatment option regardless of who actually pays. This perspective is called the *social perspective*.

Now which costs are legitimate to include from the social perspective? There is a growing consensus among health economists that it is not legitimate to include the costs of success, either medical or nonmedical. To better understand the implications of including these costs of success in a cost-effectiveness analysis, consider the following possibility:

---

■■Imagine that Simplicity's health insurance system was considering coverage of a new drug treatment for smoking cessation. The treatment itself was very inexpensive with few serious side effects. The treatment is very successful in helping patients stop smoking and dramatically reduces their probability of developing lung cancer in the future. The affect on other diseases that are increased by smoking is much smaller. Despite these advantages the authors of the cost-effectiveness study found that the costs of the smoking cessation treatment were very high. They argued that the costs of taking care of patients with rapidly fatal lung cancer was quite low compared with the costs of success. These costs include treating other chronic diseases the individuals would develop in later years.■■

---

Thus, including the costs of success can make it look very costly to keep people alive. It is assumed that lung cancer deaths are rapid and inexpensive because little can be done compared to slow and expensive deaths from other lung diseases or chronic heart diseases. Thus preventing lung cancer may look very expensive once the medical costs of success are included. If we include nonmedical costs of success such as paying for the social security of those who live longer the situation is even worse. Including nonmedical costs of success in a cost-effectiveness analysis can make it look very expensive to keep people alive even when they are healthy.

The medical and nonmedical input costs are considered the legitimate costs to add together from the social perspective. The resulting costs will be called the *net costs* Thus from the social perspective the net costs of Pneumogone are:

| | |
|---|---:|
| Production ...................... | $300 |
| Induced costs ..................... | $ 20 |
| Induced cost savings ............... | −$200 |
| Access costs ..................... | $100 |
| Disability costs ................... | −$175 |
| Total .......................... | $ 45 per use |

Thus, cost-effectiveness analysis is generally done from the social perspective of the payer using all the legitimate opportunity costs of care regardless of who actually pays the bills. The medical costs of success, and the nonmedical costs of success are not generally considered part of the net costs from the social perspective.

Now that we have examined what we are measuring when we calculate the net costs of a treatment option, let us return to the job of using cost-effectiveness analysis to implement Simplicity's health system.

# CHAPTER SEVEN

# Cost-Effectiveness: Can it Help in Choosing Treatment?

Now we are ready to use net costs from the social perspective and net benefit as measured in QALYs to help us implement the second and third basic principles of Simplicity's health system. That is:

- How can we determine which package of health services will allow us to maximize effectiveness while minimizing costs?
- How can we recognize when health services that are effective do not produce enough net benefit to be worth the net costs?

Let us begin with the frequently occurring situation in which there are several available treatments that can effectively treat a disease. In this situation we are looking for the treatment or combination of treatments which can maximize the effectiveness while at the same time minimize the cost. To examine this problem and learn how to implement the second basic principle of Simplicity's health system let us look at the next decision facing you as Head of Health.

■■Your next decision in Simplicity is to evaluate the best way to treat a common medical condition technically known as Glandular Overactivity, but usually called by its initials, GO. Standard Treatment for GO has previously consisted of watchful waiting and early treatment of complications. Symptoms which occurred before the development of complications were treated with over-the-counter medications.

Recently, two new treatments have been developed that allow effective treatment of the underlying disease prior to the development of complications. One treatment is called Laserectomy and the other is called Med-Cure. Both treatment options are capable of producing the same total number of QALYs when used on all cases of GO, but they have quite different costs.

Laserectomy costs an additional $10,000,000 to produce 1,000 QALYs. That is, when compared to Standard Treatment, Laserectomy requires additional expenditures to produce additional QALYs.

The other treatment, called Med-Cure, is very inexpensive and reduces the costs by avoiding hospitalizations for complications that would occur if Standard Treatment were chosen. Thus Med-Cure's costs are actually less than zero, because it reduces the costs from the social perspective. Med-Cure has a cost of −$1,000,000 to produce its 1,000 QALYs.                    ■■

## IS LASERECTOMY OR MED-CURE MORE COST-EFFECTIVE?

When treatments have the same costs or the same effectiveness the results of a cost-effectiveness analysis can be presented using a cost-effectiveness ratio. This is the case for Laserectomy and Med-Cure, because they provide the same number of QALYs. The cost-effectiveness ratio lets us examine one treatment option at a time and compares each option to Standard Treatment.[1]

The cost-effectiveness ratio contains the net costs in the numerator and the effectiveness (net benefit) in the denominator. Thus in our example the cost-effectiveness ratio indicates that

---

[1] The comparison in a cost-effectiveness analysis may be standard treatment, comfort care only, or no treatment at all. The comparison chosen may greatly effect the results. When new therapies are being assessed the usual comparison is the current standard therapy.

Laserectomy and Med–Cure result in the following average cost per QALY produced.

Laserectomy:

$$\frac{\$10,000,000}{1,000 \; \text{QALY}} = \frac{+\$10,000}{\text{QALY}}$$

Med–Cure:

$$\frac{-\$1,000,000}{1,000 \; \text{QALY}} = \frac{-\$1,000}{\text{QALY}}$$

Both Laserectomy and Med–Cure can produce 1,000 QALYs, but Med–Cure can produce this outcome for less cost. Thus Med–Cure is more cost-effective than Laserectomy. Med–Cure actually produces additional QALYs while reducing costs. This is a special and unusual situation. Applying the second basic principle of Simplicity's health care system we would conclude that Med–Cure should be covered and Laserectomy should not be covered. Even though Laserectomy is effective it does not maximize effectiveness while minimizing costs.

Usually the situation is not quite so simple. There are often several available therapies which need to be considered. Let us take a look at several other options for treating GO.

---

■There is a treatment option called Feel-Good. Feel-Good is a medication that treats the early symptoms of GO. Feel-Good also reduces costs by $1,000,000 compared to Standard Treatment. However, because Feel-Good effectively masks early symptoms, complications are not discovered early, resulting in more deaths and reducing the number of QALYs by 100, compared with Standard Treatment.        ■

---

The cost-effectiveness ratio of Feel-Good is:

$$\text{Feel-Good} = \frac{-\$1,000,000}{-100 \; \text{QALY}} = \frac{+\$10,000}{\text{QALY}}$$

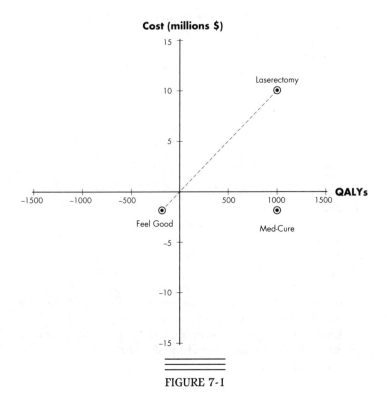

FIGURE 7-1

Thus the cost-effectiveness ratio for Feel-Good is the same as for Laserectomy. Since the costs of Feel-Good and Laserectomy are the same and the cost-effectiveness ratios are the same, you ask yourself:

IS FEEL-GOOD JUST AS COST-EFFECTIVE
AS LASERECTOMY?

Figure 7–1 displays the cost-effectiveness ratios of Laserectomy, Med-Cure, and Feel-Good on what we will call a *Cost-QALY graph*. The Cost-QALY graph has costs on the vertical axis and QALYs on the horizontal axis. The cost-effectiveness ratios are measured by the slope of the lines that connect a particular therapy to the intersection of the axes or the zero point.

Notice in figure 7-1 that Med-Cure has a negative slope

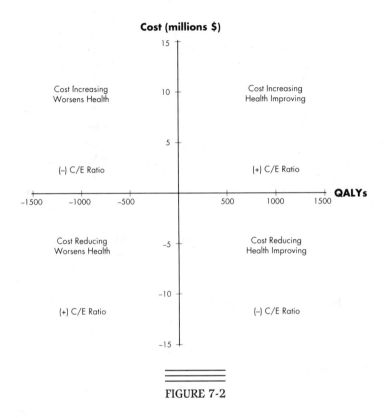

**Cost (millions $)**

Cost Increasing
Worsens Health

Cost Increasing
Health Improving

(–) C/E Ratio

(+) C/E Ratio

QALYs

Cost Reducing
Worsens Health

Cost Reducing
Health Improving

(+) C/E Ratio

(–) C/E Ratio

FIGURE 7-2

whereas Laserectomy has a positive slope. Feel-Good has the same slope as Laserectomy. However, Feel-Good lies in the lower left quarter or quadrant of the graph, whereas Laserectomy lies in the right upper quadrant.

Figure 7–2 displays the implications of each of the quadrants of the Cost-QALYs graph. In the right upper quadrant where Laserectomy lies, the costs increase, but so does health, as measured by QALYs. Thus when looking at cost-effectiveness ratios that lie in the right upper quadrant we need to ask: is the increased health worth the increased costs? Options located in the right upper quadrant can at times be considered cost-effective. Calling a right upper quadrant option such as Laserectomy cost-effective implies that we consider the additional QALYs worth the additional cost.

Feel-Good, in contrast, is located in the left lower quadrant. In this quadrant the costs are reduced but so is health. Thus, when we are looking at cost-effectiveness ratios in the left lower quadrant we need to ask: is the decreased health worth the reduced cost? Cost-effectiveness ratios located in the lower left quadrant may at times also be called cost-effective. Calling a left lower quadrant option such as Feel-Good cost-effective implies that we consider the reduced costs worth the reduced QALYs.

Thus, a positive cost-effectiveness ratio can have two very different meanings. It can imply more costs for more health or it can imply less costs for less health. Thus, when confronted with a positive cost-effectiveness ratio the question to ask is: in which quadrant?

The right lower quadrant, where Med-Cure lies, is the ideal location. In this quadrant costs are reduced while health, as measured by QALYs, is increased. This appears to be the best of both worlds. In the remaining left upper quadrant costs are increased while QALYs are reduced. This worst of all possible worlds also carries a negative sign and could possibly be confused with a cost-reducing health-improving therapy located in the right lower quadrant.[2]

Thus, even though Laserectomy and Feel-Good have the same cost-effectiveness ratio, they are not the same. If our primary goal is to maximize health, Laserectomy is clearly better than Feel-Good, even though they have the same cost-effectiveness ratio. Thus you recommend that Feel-Good not be covered for treatment of GO.

---

Recently a new option for treatment of GO (called Raybeam) was discovered that produces additional effectiveness by reducing treatment time and further reducing complications compared with Laserectomy or Med-Cure. Raybeam, like Laserectomy, has a net cost of $10,000,000 but it produces 1,500 QALYs.

---

### SHOULD RAYBEAM BE USED INSTEAD OF LASERECTOMY OR MED-CURE?

---

[2] For options like Laserectomy in the right upper quadrant, the smaller the cost-effectiveness ratio the better because here a small ratio implies low costs per QALY gained. For options such as Feel-Good in the left lower quadrant the larger the cost-effectiveness ratio the better, because here a large ratio implies a large reduction in costs for every QALY lost.

Cost-effectiveness ratios are the best single measure to use when choosing between treatment options if only one can be selected and all the options being compared (1) have the same costs, or (2) have the same effectiveness. Laserectomy and Raybeam both have the same cost, so they can be compared using the cost-effectiveness ratio, as follows:

Laserectomy:

$$\frac{\$10,000,000}{1,000 \text{ QALY}} = \frac{\$10,000}{\text{QALY}}$$

Raybeam:

$$\frac{\$10,000,000}{1,500 \text{ QALY}} = \frac{\$6,667}{\text{QALY}}$$

Thus we can say that Raybeam is *more* cost-effective than Laserectomy. Even though Raybeam is more cost-effective than Laserectomy, whether we want to label Raybeam as cost-effective and thus cover it as parts of the package of services will depend on our other options. Thus we need to compare Raybeam with Med-Cure. Figure 7–3 displays Raybeam, Laserectomy, and Med-Cure on a Cost-QALY graph.

Notice that Med-Cure does not produce as many QALYs as Raybeam, despite the fact that it increases the effectiveness while reducing the cost. Raybeam produces more QALYs for more cost than Med-Cure. Thus, we cannot use the cost-effectiveness ratio to compare Med-Cure and Raybeam.

In this situation we are really interested in calculating the additional or incremental cost per QALY required if we chose to use Raybeam and not Med-Cure. That is, we want to know what is called the *incremental cost-effectiveness ratio*. The incremental cost-effectiveness ratio tells us how much we would need to pay to achieve an additional QALY if we substituted Raybeam for Med-Cure. The incremental cost-effectiveness ratio is the measure to use to compare two or more options, when the options have different costs and also result in different numbers of QALYs.

An incremental cost-effectiveness ratio can be calculated as follows:

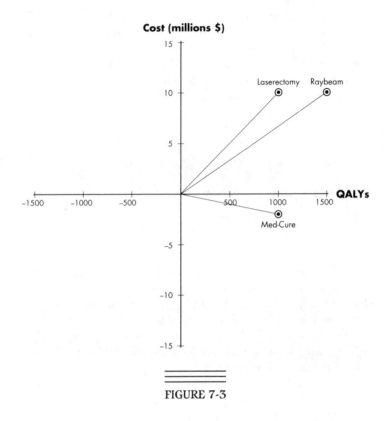

FIGURE 7-3

$$\frac{\text{Cost Raybeam} - \text{Cost Med-Cure}}{\text{Effectiveness Raybeam} - \text{Effectiveness Med-Cure}} =$$

$$\frac{\$10,000,000 - (-\$1,000,000)}{1,500 \text{ QALYs} - 1,000 \text{ QALYs}} = \frac{\$11,000,000}{500 \text{ QALYs}} = \frac{\$22,000}{\text{QALY}}$$

This incremental cost-effectiveness ratio of $22,000/QALY indicates the additional cost of obtaining a QALY if we substitute Raybeam for Med-Cure. Figure 7–4 displays the incremental cost-effectiveness ratio as well as the cost-effectiveness ratios for Raybeam and Med-Cure. The incremental cost-effectiveness ra-

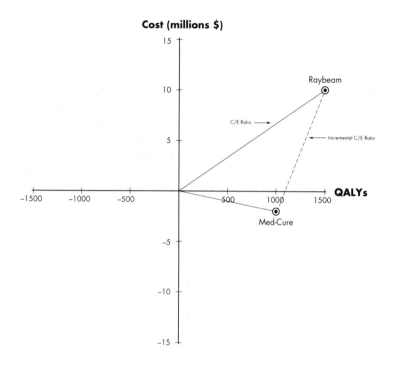

Med-Cure = C/E Ratio = −$1,000 / QALY

Raybeam = C/E Ratio = $6,667 / QALY

Incremental C/E ratio = $22,000 / QALY

FIGURE 7-4

tio is measured by the slope of the dotted line connecting Med-Cure with Raybeam.

Notice that the incremental cost-effectiveness ratio of obtaining the additional QALY obtained by substituting Raybeam for Med-Cure is substantially higher than the previous cost-effectiveness ratios obtained. It is often the case that incremental cost-effectiveness ratios will be higher than cost-effectiveness ratios. Thus, it is important to distinguish between them and avoid comparing cost-effectiveness ratios which compare average costs to achieve a QALY, with incremental cost-effectiveness ratios which ask about the additional cost to achieve an additional QALY. In general, we can obtain the best understanding of the options if cost-effectiveness ratios and, when needed, incremental cost-effectiveness ratios are presented.

Why are we only comparing one treatment to another? Aren't there some ways to use one, the other, or both depending on the situation? Couldn't we save money and increase QALYs by combining treatments? Under Simplicity's health system this type of situation comes up frequently. It is dealt with by developing what are called *clinical guidelines*. Clinical guidelines in Simplicity are a formal recommendation process which has gradually come to have legal, as well as reimbursement, implications. Clinical guidelines provide three levels of recommendations known as (1) *standards,* (2) *guidelines,* and (3) *options.*[3]

A recommendation as a standard implies that a therapy should be performed on all patients with a particular condition. Standards are only approved if an assessment of the probabilities and the utilities of the group indicate that the decision to choose the treatment would be virtually unanimous. In addition, a standard implies that the treatment is considered cost-effective for those for whom it is being recommended. Standards can also be approved if the decision of a group of individuals with the condition would be virtually unanimous to refuse the treatment or if the decision has been made not to pay for the treatment because there are no groups of individuals for whom the treatment can be considered cost-effective.

A recommendation as a guideline implies that a substantial majority of the individuals in a group prefer one treatment. Recommendations as a guideline implies that a minority of individuals with the condition favor other alternatives after considering the probabilities and utilities. In addition, before a treatment is recommended in the form of a guideline it must be considered cost-effective. The guidelines may include a list of the factors that

---

[3] The term *guideline* is used in two somewhat different ways. Clinical guideline refers to the entire set of recommendations of which a guideline is one specific type. In addition the term *standard* should not be confused with *standard care.*

have been found to affect the choice. These factors include special situations that increase the probability of reduced benefit such as the presence of other diseases. They also include situations which increase the probability of harm such as an increased concern over a potential side effect. Guidelines imply that there are more than one alternative that can in special circumstances be recommended to patients and may be preferred by patients.

A recommendation as an option implies that there is no single alternative that would be chosen by a clear majority of patients with the condition after taking into account the probabilities and utilities. Options imply that individuals often differ in their choice of treatment and no general recommendations for the group are possible. Options may also be included when the data on benefits, harms, or costs are not adequate to develop guidelines or standards.

> ▬You decide to look into these questions and ask the experts on Glandular Overactivity and cost-effectiveness analysis to meet and develop a set of clinical guidelines for treating GO. Several months later you receive a brief summary labeled *A Guide to the Guidelines for Treating GO*. The summary reads as follows:
> Standard: Feel-Good should not be used as a treatment for Glandular Overactivity.
> Guidelines: Treatment of Glandular Overactivity should generally begin with Med-Cure. One-third of patients will fail to respond to Med-Cure. These patients should be treated with Raybeam. Research is currently in progress to identify special situations in which Med-Cure is likely to fail and where Raybeam should be used first. Until those results provide evidence that they are cost-effective, using Med-Cure as the initial treatment for everyone is considered the most cost-effective approach.            ▬

**WILL YOU RECOMMEND APPROVAL OF THESE CLINICAL GUIDELINES FOR TREATING GO?**

Under these clinical guidelines, all individuals with GO are treated with Med-Cure to obtain a total of 1,000 QALYs for a cost of −\$1,000,000; that is a cost savings. After using Med-Cure on everyone it is possible to utilize Raybeam on the one-third of patients who do not receive the benefit from Med-Cure.[4]

Use of Raybeam on the one-third of patients who fail Med-Cure should produce one-third of the 1,500 QALYs it produces if used on everyone. Thus, use of Raybeam on those in which Med-Cure fails would produce 500 additional QALYs. The cost per QALY for Raybeam is \$6,667; therefore, the cost of use of Raybeam is:

$$\frac{(500 \text{ QALYs})(\$6,667)}{\text{QALY}} = \$3,333,500$$

Let us call this new approach Med-Cure/Raybeam and calculate the cost-effectiveness ratio from this combined approach.

Because Med-Cure reduces the cost by \$1,000,000 and use of Raybeam on those who fail Med-Cure costs an additional \$3,333,500, the net cost of Med-Cure/Raybeam is \$2,333,500 (i.e., \$3,333,500 − \$1,000,000). Use of Med-Cure/Raybeam produces a total of 1,500 QALYs. Thus, the overall cost-effectiveness ratio for this combination is:

$$\frac{\$2,333,500}{1500 \text{ QALYs}} = \frac{\$1,556}{\text{QALY}}$$

Figure 7–5 displays the Med-Cure/Raybeam alternative as well as the Med-Cure and the Raybeam alternatives that indicate use of these treatments as the only therapies. Med-Cure/Raybeam produces the same number of QALYs as Raybeam alone, but at far less average cost (cost-effectiveness ratios \$1,556/QALY versus \$6,667/QALY).

Thus, Med-Cure followed by Raybeam can be recommended treatment because it produces the maximum possible number of QALYs and does it for the least possible cost. Thus according to the second principle of Simplicity's health system this is the best approach. Nonetheless, some patients and some

---

[4]In making these calculations it is assumed that Raybeam, used after Med-Cure fails, has the same effect that it would have had if used initially on these patients. That is, we are making the independence assumption that success or failure with Med-Cure does not influence the success or failure with Raybeam.

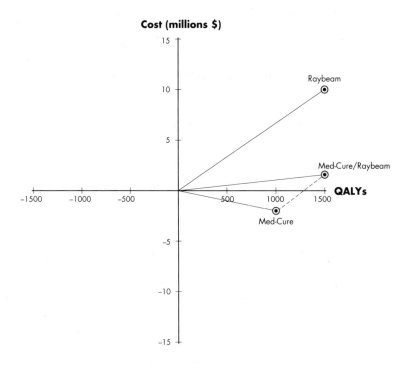

Raybeam C/E ratio = $6,667 / QALY

Med-Cure/Raybeam C/E ratio = $1,555 / QALY

FIGURE 7-5

clinicians may prefer to use Raybeam or even Laserectomy first. If you adopt these clinical guidelines these approaches would not generally be covered because they are not recommended except perhaps in special situations.

Your decision to recommend approval of these clinical guidelines may influence greatly how GO is treated in Simplicity. Based on Simplicity's second basic principle you decide to recommend these clinical guidelines even though you recognize that they will restrict the treatment choices for patients and for clinicians.

Maybe we can do even better if we learn to predict who is likely to fail Med-Cure and should be initially started on Raybeam.

When we have more than one effective treatment we need to look carefully to see if there are ways to combine the alternatives. Our GO example suggests that some therapies can be held in reserve and used only if needed. At other times it may be possible to use one form of treatment on one type of patient and a different treatment alternative on other types of patients. This approach may make sense from the standpoint of effectiveness as well as financial costs.

In our GO example it was possible to achieve maximum effectiveness, and the issue was one of minimizing cost to accomplish that goal. Unfortunately this is not always the case. In these situations the third operating principle of Simplicity's health system goes into effect and we need to ask: how can we recognize when health services that are effective do not produce enough net benefit to be worth the net cost?

Remember what happens in Simplicity when it is decided that the net benefit is not worth the net cost. The additional health services above-and-beyond those covered in the package may then be purchased by individuals out-of-pocket when they receive the services or through purchase of additional insurance.

Let us see how this third principle operates by taking a look at the next issue you face as Head of Health.

---

Just as you finish deciding to recommend the clinical guidelines for treatment of GO, a new report appears and is rapidly broadcast by the news media.

Your decision to provide prevention for Paralysis but not Coronary has resulted in 10,000 cases per year of Coronary. Half these individuals ignore the early symptoms of Coronary and die each year before they can reach medical care. The other 5,000 reach medical care and require treatment.

Suddenly you are faced with a new crisis: you must decide what to do about those people in whom Coronary develops. For individuals in Simplicity in whom Coronary develops and who reach treatment there have been two treatments available, either of which could be used as the sole treatment for all patients with Coronary. The treatments have the following net costs and net benefits:

Basic Care: $10,000 per use produces an average of 2 additional QALYs per use

Comprehensive Care: $20,000 per use produces an average of 3 additional QALYs per use ▬

## WILL YOU RECOMMEND COMPREHENSIVE CARE OR BASIC CARE?

The cost-effectiveness ratio for Basic Care is:

$$\frac{\$10,000}{2 \text{ QALYs}} = \frac{\$5,000}{\text{QALY}}$$

The cost-effectiveness ratio for Comprehensive Care is:

$$\frac{\$20,000}{3 \text{ QALYs}} = \frac{\$6,667}{\text{QALY}}$$

Comprehensive Care is more expensive per QALY than Basic Care, but it also provides more QALYs. Thus, we should also calculate the incremental cost-effectiveness ratio, which tells us the cost per additional or incremental QALY.

The incremental cost-effectiveness ratio is calculated as follows:

$$\frac{\text{Cost Comprehensive Care} - \text{Cost Basic Care}}{\text{QALYs Comprehensive Care} - \text{QALYs Basic Care}}$$

$$\frac{\$20,000 - \$10,000}{3 \text{ QALYs} - 2 \text{ QALYs}} = \frac{\$10,000}{\text{QALY}}$$

Now we are forced to ask the question: is the net benefit worth the net cost? Thus we must ask if a QALY is worth $10,000.

Fortunately in Simplicity we know the cost per QALY of all our health services; $10,000 per QALY is below the $15,000 average that we pay for an additional QALY. In Simplicity there is a rule of thumb that states: if the incremental cost-effectiveness ratio is no more than the average of previously approved incremental cost-effectiveness ratios then it will be approved automatically. However, if it is more than the average it will only be approved after specifically considering whether the net benefit is worth the net cost.

Fortunately you do not need to consider whether Comprehensive Care is worth the additional cost. The fact that $10,000 is less than the average for previously approved therapies providing additional QALYs implies that Simplicity will automatically provide coverage for Comprehensive Care for Coronary as part of the package of health services. Thus you recommend that Comprehensive Care be provided for all patients in Simplicity who need medical care for Coronary.

---

■Just as you think this issue is resolved, the newest issue of the Old England Journal of Medicine announces the newest technological advance in the treatment of Coronary. The treatment has been called Cardiomagic. Cardiomagic has the following cost and QALYs: $120,000 per use that produces an average of 5 additional QALYs per use.                                            ■

---

## WOULD YOU RECOMMEND COMPREHENSIVE CARE OR CARDIOMAGIC FOR TREATMENT OF PATIENTS WITH CORONARY?

At first you are delighted to hear of this new advance in therapy. Cardiomagic produces 5 additional QALYs per use, compared with 3 additional QALYs per use for Comprehensive Care. Now maybe we can treat all 5,000 people who present for care with Coronary and produce an additional 2 QALYs per use.

However, to treat everyone who presents for care with Coronary with Cardiomagic would cost Simplicity the following:

$$\begin{array}{c}(\$120,000 \text{ per use}) \times \\ (5,000 \text{ reaching care for Coronary})\end{array} = \$600,000,000.$$

Thus we need to determine how much each additional QALY costs. To do this we calculate an incremental cost-effectiveness ratio, comparing Cardiomagic with Comprehensive Care.

$$\text{Incremental Cost-effectiveness ratio} = \frac{\$120{,}000 - \$20{,}000}{5 \text{ QALYs} - 3 \text{ QALYs}} = \frac{\$50{,}000}{\text{QALY}}$$

The incremental cost-effectiveness ratio provides the best estimate of what Simplicity really needs to pay, on average, for each of those extra QALYs that Cardiomagic provides. Now at least you know what it costs to produce an additional QALY using Cardiomagic. However, before you make a recommendation we need to recognize that cost estimates, just like harms or benefit estimates, contain uncertainties. In harm–benefit analysis these uncertainties are often dealt with using a sensitivity analysis. The same general approach is also applicable to cost-effectiveness analysis.

Sensitivity analysis in cost-effectiveness analysis is performed employing the same approaches used in harm–benefit analysis. Realistic high and realistic low estimates for factors which are not certain can be estimated. These high or low estimates can then be used to recalculate cost-effectiveness or incremental cost-effectiveness ratios.

There is always some doubt about the accurracy of cost estimates in a cost-effectiveness analysis. However, after studying the issue, you realize that the greatest uncertainty is how many people will seek care if Cardiomagic is available. Perhaps the use of Cardiomagic will convice individuals with Coronary to seek care for those symptoms that in the past individuals often ignored. Therefore, it may be necessary to make a high estimate of the number of individuals who will reach medical care for Coronary.

----

■■After the publicity regarding Cardiomagic, you estimate that there will be an increase to 7,500 individuals per year, from the 10,000 that experience a Coronary, who will reach medical care for Coronary. This compares to 5,000 who currently reach medical care. In this new situation the total costs won't be $600,000,000; rather they will be $900,000,000. However, we can assume that these additional individuals will also obtain

additional QALYs. Thus, the incremental cost-effectiveness
ratio will still be approximately $50,000 per QALY.
Now you have to address the question directly:              ▬

## IN SIMPLICITY IS A QALY WORTH $50,000?

This is the question you were afraid you would have to answer.
Now you need to put a monetary value on a year of healthy life:
on a QALY. Cost-effectiveness analysis is used most of the time
in the analysis of the economic consequences of health decisions
because it allows us to escape answering the difficult question,
what is a QALY worth? By avoiding that final and difficult step
we also have in practice isolated health care decisions from other
potential alternative uses of money. We do not need to ask,
would the money be better spend for education or for recreation?

Many health economists would prefer to use what they call
*cost-benefit analysis*. In cost-benefit analysis QALYs are converted
to monetary units such as dollars. If this can be done it allows us
to make comparisons between spending money to produce
QALYs and spending it in other ways.[5]

When converting QALYs to dollars in a cost-benefit analysis
we use the social perspective. This allows us to avoid having to
ask what any one particular person's QALY is worth. It still
requires that we ask what the average QALY is worth.

Even if you think converting QALYs into dollars is a good
idea, the dollar figure to place on a QALY remains very controver-
sial. One approach used by health economists is called the *human
capital* approach. In one form of the human capital approach, the
financial benefit of a QALY is measured in terms of the average
economic productivity that an additional QALY allows to take
place. The human capital approach has been criticized because it

---

[5] A cost-benefit analysis may not directly place a value on a QALY. Rather it
would go back to the data on outcomes and put dollars on each of the outcomes. These dollar amounts would then be added. This process allows a
dollar value to be derived for the average QALY. Also note that the use of the
term *benefit* here is not the same as when used in a harm-benefit analysis. Here
benefit implies that we have converted what we have called effectiveness (i.e.,
benefits minus harms) into monetary units (dollars). Cost-benefit analysis implies that both the costs of providing the care and the effectiveness are measured in the same monetary units, such as dollars.

does not include any considerations except economic productivity, as reflected in wages. This approach implies that the contribution of those outside the work force are not included in calculating the total value of the QALYs.

There are other approaches that actually try to determine the value a society places on the additional QALYs. One approach, known as the *willingness-to-pay* approach, tries to estimate how much a society is willing to pay to provide an additional QALY based on the society's actual choices in previous situations. This approach has been very difficult to implement and has not been widely used. Many economists, however, favor the concept incorporated into the willingness–to-pay approach.[6]

---

▬In Simplicity and many other communities, a financial value is not usually placed on a QALY. Rather, a cap or upper limit is set on the total amount of money that can be spent for covered health services. Within this overall limit the decisions to cover or not cover specific services have to be made. This process of deciding which services will be covered in effect determines the value that the community places on a QALY.

In Simplicity after much debate, many coverage decisions, and more than a little soul searching, it has been accepted that for purposes of cost-benefit analysis a QALY will be converted to $30,000.                                     ▬

---

## SHOULD CARDIOMAGIC BE COVERED AS PART OF THE PACKAGE OF COST EFFECTIVE HEALTH SERVICES?

The incremental cost-effectiveness ratio for Cardiomagic is $50,000 per QALY. Thus you are tempted to conclude that Simplicity should not cover Cardiomagic as part of the package of cost-effective services. Since Cardiomagic has been shown to be effective (even if it is not regarded as cost-effective) it will

---

[6] The willingness-to-pay approach here assumes that the willingness-to-pay is an average for society since willingness-to-pay on the individual level is greatly affected by the amount of money an individual has to spend.

fall under the third basic principle of Simplicity's health care system. That is, the citizens of Simplicity will be allowed to purchase Cardiomagic out-of-pocket when they receive the services, or through additional insurance.

This is a decision you don't want to make. If you declare that Cardiomagic will not be provided as part of the package of cost-effective services you clearly will be denying some individuals the advantages of Cardiomagic. For them, use of Cardiomagic would on average maximize their net benefit. Those who suffer a Coronary are faced with paying for Cardiomagic themselves—out-of-pocket—or accepting Comprehensive Care. The choice that individuals make at this point is heavily influenced by their ability to pay. The affluent are much more likely to choose to receive Cardiomagic.

Back in the 1990s when the health care system of Simplicity was reformed, this issue was actively debated. The system which emerged guaranteed everyone in Simplicity coverage for all care which was considered cost-effective. (i.e., all care whose additional QALYs were considered worth their additional cost). This was a major improvement.

Individuals in Simplicity were still allowed to pay for additional care, above and beyond the covered services, either out-of-pocket or by purchasing additional insurance coverage. Thus in practice Simplicity accepted a system in which those who had more money could decide to receive additional services that were not considered by Simplicity to be cost-effective. Just like purchasing an automobile, more financial resources make it easier to purchase a more expensive car. However, with health care there are a number of other factors that influence the decision.[7]

This compromise reflected the philosophy and realities of Simplicity. Those with additional resources sought to preserve their right to spend those resources on additional effective health services.

You have concerns about limiting the use of Cardiomagic to

---

[7] The cost also differs if the service is paid for out-of-pocket at the time of service or through additional insurance. The choice by individuals to pay for Cardiomagic through additional insurance will depend heavily on how the insurance is structured, including what other services are covered and how many (and what type) of individuals participate. Thus we will deal with the more straightforward situation where the entire cost is covered out-of-pocket at the time the service is received.

those who pay for it themselves. You recognize that this implies that those with more money have the opportunity to purchase additional effective health services. Is there any way out of this bind? Not completely. However, it may be possible to identify a smaller group of patients who are really the ones who would benefit the most from Cardiomagic. If we can learn more about what affects outcomes or prognosis then we could better predict what will happen to groups of individuals. If, for instance, those with more severe disease or those with acute onset are the ones who gain the greatest benefit from Cardiomagic, then for these groups the effectiveness of the therapy will be increased and for these groups Cardiomagic may be considered cost-effective. It may then be possible to provide coverage for Cardiomagic in the package of services using a guideline that limits the use of Cardiomagic to those who benefit the most.

You decide to recommend future coverage for Cardiomagic for those groups of patients whose incremental cost–effectiveness is shown, on the basis of future studies, to be less than $30,000. For other groups of patients you decide to allow then to pay for Cardiomagic themselves—either out of their pockets or through their own private health insurance. For now, that means more research. Increasing effectiveness, reducing costs, and better predictions of outcomes are the only way out of the bind in which we find ourselves. As a result of your decision, not everyone will receive maximum potential benefit; however, at least Simplicity will be paying for Cardiomagic to help those who could potentially benefit the most.

Now we have seen the ways the cost-effectiveness system works in Simplicity, based on each of the three basic principles. According to the first principle, when we are constrained by a fixed budget (such as for preventive services), cost-effectiveness analysis can help us decide how to obtain the greatest effectiveness within the budget.

According to the second principle, when there are several choices of therapy and we desire to maximize effectiveness while minimizing cost (such as when considering inclusion of services in the covered package), we can use cost-effectiveness ratios as a basis for deciding which option or combination of options is most cost-effective.

According to the third principle, when we wish to determine whether the net benefit is worth the net cost (such as when deciding whether to cover Cardiomagic), we can use cost-benefit analysis to help us see clearly the trade-offs we need to make.

Now you are almost ready to apply the basic principles of Simplicity's cost-effectiveness system. However, first we need to consider one additional factor. We need to take into account the timing of the benefits, harms, and costs.

# CHAPTER EIGHT

## Discounting Costs
## and Effectiveness

As you take a few minutes to think about the recommendations you have made so far, you realize that you have been acting as if all the benefits, all the harms, and all the costs occurred in the immediate future. In cost-effectiveness analysis, as in harm-benefit analysis, some of the consequences of the alternatives we choose do not occur immediately. Side effects of drugs may be delayed, benefits of prevention may not be apparent for years, and the costs of treatment may extend over decades. Thus, it is necessary to take the timing of benefits, harms, and costs into account by a process health economists call *discounting*.

Before looking at what discounting implies in cost-effectiveness analysis, how it is performed, and how it can effect the results of cost-effectiveness analysis, let us take a look at what discounting is not. Discounting is not an effort to take inflation into account. Inflation is taken into account in a cost-effectiveness analysis by making all calculations in "today's" dollars, yen, marks, pounds, pesos or other currency. Economists call these *constant dollars*. The rate of inflation is extremely difficult to predict and extremely variable from year to year and country to country.

Thus economists have traditionally made their calculations in constant dollars.

Discounting is designed to take into account the timing of events. It is the same phenomenon that occurred when we examined harms and benefits. A benefit in the future is worth less than a benefit now, and a harm delayed is not as bad as a harm now. Those future benefits from controlling hypertension need to be quite large to sacrifice physical endurance or potency now. Similarly, fears of secondary cancer from chemotherapy in the future may seem incidental compared with current benefits.

Costs must also be discounted. Most people would prefer to receive $100 dollars today rather than $100 one year from now. If you receive the $100 today you generally can safely invest it and receive what economists call a *real rate of return*. A real rate of return provides you with more than $100 one year from now (even after adjusting for inflation).

Looked at the other way around, most people would prefer to pay $100 one year from now rather than pay it today. Delaying payment for one year allows you to invest the money and receive a real rate of return. Thus, money spent in the future is not as "costly" as money spent now. Economists calculate the amount of money that needs to be put aside today to pay bills that are not due until future years. In this process we are discounting costs. This amount of money which needs to be put aside today is called the *discounted present value* or *present value*. Thus, when including costs that do not need to be paid until a future date, a cost–effectiveness analysis should discount the costs and calculate the present value.[1]

When we are discounting costs at 3% we only need to put aside $100 today to pay for a $103 obligation which must be paid one year form now. Extending this into the future the $100 will be enough to cover a cost of $106.09 that does not need to be paid for two years. This number is obtained by the following calculations.

---

[1] Economists continue to argue among themselves about the best discount rate, including whether the discount rate used for health programs should be different from other programs. A 3 or 4% discount rate is often acceptable for a cost-effectiveness analysis, though some economists prefer a 5% rate. Performance of a sensitivity analysis with costs and effectiveness discounted from 0 to 5% is frequently recommended. Most economists argue that benefits, harms and costs should be discounted at the same rate. If benefits are discounted at a lower rate there is always a reason to delay purchasing an option that produces benefits because the benefits will be relatively cheaper to purchase in the future.

For the first year:

$$(\$100) + (.03)(\$100) = \$103$$

For the second year:

$$(\$103) + (.03)(\$103) = \$106.09$$

We can extend this process as far as we wish into the future. Often, however, discounting is actually performed in reverse. That is, we know that we will need $103 next year; therefore we need $100 in present value to cover that amount in one year.[2]

Unless you are going to be the one performing the discounting procedure, the most important thing to understand is the consequences of discounting for the recommendations of cost-effectiveness analysis. Thus we will take a look at a series of cost-effectiveness analyses and answer the following question for each cost–effectiveness analysis.[3]

## WHAT IS THE IMPACT THAT DISCOUNTING COSTS, BENEFITS, AND HARMS WILL HAVE ON THE RESULTS?

1. Treating seizures in which costs, benefits, and harms all occur with approximately the same timing.
2. Using an effective short-term treatment for cigarette cessation that has side effects and thus harms in the short-run as well as costs but substantial benefits that begin immediately and continue for many years.
3. Providing vaccinations to infants that produces rare but serious side effects and costs in the short-run but prevents a common and serious illness during their teenage years.
4. Medication with no serious side effects that delays the development of cataracts and allows surgery with its increased costs and poetential harms to be delayed an average of 5 years.

---

[2]The formula for discounting is: Present value = dollars owed in n years/$(1 + r)^n$ where r = discount rate and n = number of years in the future. Thus the present value of $106.09 is calculated as $106.09/$(1 + .03)(1 + .03)$ = $100.

[3] In these analyses we assume that the treatment is effective in increasing the number of QALYs and that the costs also increase. Thus, we are dealing with treatment options located in the right upper quadrant of the Cost-QALY graph where the smaller the cost-effectiveness ratio the better.

## Seizures

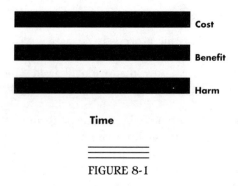

FIGURE 8-1

## Smoking Cessation

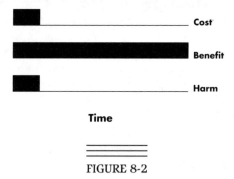

FIGURE 8-2

Figure 8–1 shows the timing of occurrence of the costs, benefits, and harms of treating. Discounting will affect all three in the same way regardless of the discount rate used. Thus, discounting does not affect the results of this cost-effectiveness analysis.

Figure 8–2 shows the timing of costs, benefits, and harms

## Vaccination

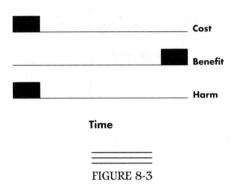

FIGURE 8-3

of smoking cessation. The costs and harms occur in the short-run and thus are not affected by discounting. The benefits, in contrast, extend over many years and can be substantially affected by discounting. The reduction in benefits that results from discounting will reduce the effectiveness of treatment and thus increase the cost per QALY (i.e., it will increase the cost-effectiveness ratio). The higher the discount rate the more the benefits will appear to be reduced, and the more the cost-effectiveness ratio will appear to increase, making this treatment look less attractive.

Figure 8–3 shows the timing of costs, benefits, and harms of the vaccination. This pattern is similar to smoking cessation except that the benefits do not begin until a number of years later. In this situation, the influence of discounting is even greater. Discounting benefits that only occur in the future will greatly reduce the apparent effectiveness of treatment in the denominator and thus increase the cost-effectiveness ratio. The higher the discount rate, the more the cost-effectiveness ratio will increase, making this treatment look less attractive.

Figure 8–4 shows the timing of costs, benefits, and harms for the treatment that delays the development of cataracts. This pattern is quite different from the previous ones. Here the impact of discounting is on costs and harm. By delaying the substantial cost

## Cataract

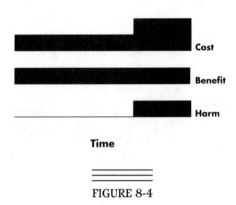

FIGURE 8-4

of surgery for 5 years, we can reduce the present value of the costs, thus reducing the numerator. The harms of surgery are also delayed and need to be discounted. Harms are subtracted from benefits in the denominator. Discounting harms makes the reduction smaller, and thus makes the denominator larger. The smaller numerator and larger denominator which result from discounting produces a smaller cost-effectiveness ratio or a smaller cost per QALY, thus making this treatment look more attractive.

The effect on the cost-effectiveness ratio in the cataract example is opposite to the effect of discounting seen in the previous two examples. Thus, discounting may make a treatment look either more or less cost-effective, depending on the timing of occurrence of costs, benefits, and harms.

# CHAPTER NINE

# Putting Cost-Effectiveness Into Practice

Now you feel ready to begin reading the cost-effectiveness literature. When you look in almost any issue of the Old England Journal of Medicine you find a cost-effectiveness analysis. One day you encounter the following situation.

---

■As the Head of Health in Simplicity you are always on the lookout for new ways to contend with the continuing SADS epidemic. One day in 2006 you read a cost-effectiveness analysis of a new treatment for SADS being investigated at University and Big City Hospitals. The treatment has been so successful that clinicians have begun to call the new therapy Better-By-Far.

You are very impressed by the cost-effectiveness analysis. Costs have been carefully calculated; effectiveness has been measured in QALYs; discounting for harms, benefits, and costs has been done using a 3% discount rate; and a sensitivity analysis has been performed.

You are quite impressed by the potential advantages of Better-By-Far if it can be used in Community Hospital and

---

other health care settings in Simplicity. Before making that recommendation, you decide to learn as much as you can about the details of implementing Better-By-Far.

You find out that Better-By-Far differs from Restrict which is currently the therapy offered at Community Hospital, in several ways.

1. Better-By-Far has greater effectiveness than Restrict. Extensive evaluation concludes that 90% of patients with SADS are cured, (i.e., they return to a quality of health of 1 on the utility scale). No side effects have resulted in any reduction in the quality of health among the first 3,000 patients. Thus, the investigators estimate the expected utility of Better-By-Far to be approximately .90, compared with .81 or less for Restrict. The investigators realize that there may be rare but serious side effects that will eventually be seen with Better-By-Far. However, using the rule of 3 they argue that these side effects are unlikely to occur more than one time per 1,000. Even if these side effects result in immediate death and thus produce a utility of 0 the expected utility of Better-By-Far would still be .899.

2. Better-By-Far has a cost-effectiveness ratio of $2,000/QALY which is the same as Restrict. However, Better-By-Far can produce additional QALYs. Its incremental cost-effectiveness ratio compared to Restrict is also $2,000. These figures are based on the 3,000 patients treated at University and Big City Hospitals. Costs may be reduced with expected improvements in Better-by-Far's techniques.

3. Better-By-Far is able to reduce costs because much of the therapy can be done on an outpatient basis; thus when put into practice, costs will be reduced and the reimbursement will be reduced.

4. Better-By-Far requires new and expensive equipment purchases; however, as compared to Restrict the equipment costs only 80% as much. Unfortunately, a critical part may fail rapidly in 20% of purchases and then requires repurchase of a new unit. Thus, on average, the cost of equipment for Better-By-Far and Restrict are the same.

5. Better-By-Far requires a period of training similar in length to that required to perform Restrict. Unfortunately, the training for Restrict is not of use in providing Better-By-Far.

6. Patients receiving Better-By-Far go through a critical period during which 10% of patients die even with the best of care. Patients need to be hospitalized during that period

> and receive around-the-clock attention from residents or attending physicians. With Restrict, the treatment must be administered on an inpatient basis, but side effects can be monitored by routine hospital visits and laboratory tests.▬

Knowing all this, you are still impressed with the potential of Better-By-Far. At the least, you expect it to produce more QALYs at the same average price per QALY. As new improvements in care occur you have reason to hope that it will reduce the cost while increasing the QALYs, which would put it in the right lower quadrant of our Cost-QALY graph (that rare but sought after combination of decreased cost and increased effectiveness). Armed with this study you set out to convince Community Hospital to change from using Restrict to using Better-By-Far. Before you can apply this study to Community Hospital you need to know as much as possible about how Community Hospital operates.

> ▬Community Hospital, unlike University and Big City Hospitals, has no residents. The hospital is an inpatient facility only. It relies on its attending physicians to provide outpatient services. Only 200 patients with SADS are treated each year. Community Hospital has operated with a surplus every year, but their surplus has declined and there is concern that they may lose money for the first time in the next year. Community Hospital invested in the equipment and staff to support the use of Restrict when it first became available. The equipment is now paid for and the staff feel competent in handling treatment using Restrict.   ▬

## WHAT FACTORS WILL COMMUNITY HOSPITAL TAKE INTO ACCOUNT IN MAKING ITS DECISION? WILL COMMUNITY HOSPITAL VOLUNTARILY AGREE TO CHANGE FROM RESTRICT TO BETTER-BY-FAR?

The institutional-provider perspective, such as that of a hospital, can be very different from the social-payer perspective of a cost-effectiveness analysis for two basic reasons. As a provider of services, Community Hospital needs to consider the impact that the new approach will have on the income to the institution. What may be good for the average institution, or even society as a whole, may not be good for Community Hospital.

In addition, the data used in a cost-effectiveness analysis may be based on assumptions that do not hold true for this particular institution. Thus we have to look very closely at where and how the data was collected and what assumptions were made before the results are accepted or extrapolated to Community Hospital.

Community Hospital's perspective may differ from the social perspective or the perspective of society as a whole in at least the following ways.

- The perspective of a hospital is that of a single provider. The hospital is interested in the prices it can charge and the resulting revenue. If reimbursement is reduced, it may be good for society as a whole but it may be bad from the perspective of the hospital budget.
- As a hospital that does not operate an outpatient facility, Community Hospital does not receive all of the revenue from Better-by-Far. Financial decision are made by institutions on the basis of revenue received relative to expenses. If the institution does not receive the revenue then for the hospital the revenue does not exist.
- Cost-effectiveness analysis takes a long-term perspective. Short-term investments in equipment and training are assumed to be spread out over the useful lifetime of the training and equipment. From Community Hospital's perspective, the previous investment in equipment and training is usually thought of as what are called *fixed costs*. Thus, institutional assessment of costs may include past commitments that are not fully considered from the social perspective of a cost-effectiveness analysis.[1]
- Short-term considerations such as the institution's yearly surplus or deficit may dominate the concern of institutions. Concerns with cash flow in the short-run can be

---

[1] Expected utility calculations of harms and benefits are made assuming that the institutions' decisions made in the past should not be considered in calculating future harms and benefits. As an extension of this principle, cost-effectiveness analysis also assumes that past costs should not be included in calculating future costs. These past costs are often called *sunk costs*.

important to institutions if it jeopardizes the confidence others have in the institution. Cost-effectiveness analysis does not usually need to concern itself with institutional stability. Institutional administrators, however, often have concerns with reputation and stability at the top of their agendas.

- Cost-effectiveness is concerned with averages. Thus uncertainties like the useful lifetime of the equipment are merely averaged in. From the institutional perspective purchases that carry uncertainty are inherently undesirable because their institution may be the ones who have to absorb the repurchase of equipment. What looks certain from a social perspective may look quite uncertain from an institutional perspective.

In addition to the differences between the social and institutional perspective, Community Hospital is organized very differently from University or Big City Hospitals where the study on Better-By-Far was conducted. Thus Community Hospital would be concerned about the impact of the following.

- Providers of care (institutions or individual providers) often concern themselves with the impact of a treatment option on their own quality of life. If Better-By-Far requires around-the-clock care by attending physicians, it will not be viewed as a desirable treatment compared with a treatment that can be administered on a routine basis.

- Cost-effectiveness analysis in theory includes the cost of the resources used. If attending physicians' time must be substituted for resident time available at Big City and University Hospitals then the cost-effectiveness ratio may not be as favorable at Community Hospital.

- The large number of patients with SADS at University and Big City Hospitals may mean that there are economies of scale when using Better-By-Far. When the treatment is used at Community Hospital, the smaller number of patients may result in higher costs per patient treated.

Thus despite the presence of a well conducted cost-effectiveness analysis of Better-By-Far, you should not be surprised to find considerable resistance to its use by Community Hospital. You now can see the difficulties of extrapolating the results of a cost-effectiveness analysis done from the social perspective of the payer of care to the institutional perspective of a particular provider of care.

Whenever a study is conducted in one particular place using one particular approach, you have to be very careful when you extrapolate or apply the results to a different setting. You have to examine the hidden or explicit assumptions made in the study and see if they hold true in the new setting. Let us look at some examples to give you practice examining these assumptions.

First let us examine some hidden assumptions related to how we measure costs. When extrapolating to new settings or expanding a program even in the same setting, the costs may change, as illustrated in the following example.

---

■■A vaccination program was found to have a cost of $50,000 and produced 10 QALYS when used on 10,000 children in one city. This city found that when the vaccination program was expanded to another 10,000 children, the costs were $40,000 to produce 10 additional QALYs. Encouraged by the reduced cost per QALY, the city confidently expanded the program to all 30,000 children, only to find that the additional 10 QALYS cost $70,000.■■

---

When the results of a cost–effectiveness analysis are extrapolated from a program of one size to a program of another size, the cost and effectiveness may change. The term *marginal costs* refers to the cost per additional QALY when the same program is expanded. This term needs to be distinguished from incremental costs, which refer to the cost per QALY when comparing one program with another, as is done in an incremental cost-effectiveness ratio. The increase in costs that occur with increase in the size of a particular program are called marginal costs.[2]

When a program is expanded it often encounters what economists call *economies of scale* and *diseconomies of scale*. Economies of scale imply that for some activities there is greater efficiency

---

[2] Not all economists make this distinction. The terms incremental costs and marginal costs are sometimes used as synonyms.

associated with greater size. An enlargened program may be able to reach people more efficiently through the mass media or may save money by buying supplies at bulk rates. Frequently, however, there is a point at which size becomes a problem and diseconomies of scale occur. For instance, new participants may be harder to reach or personnel may not be used efficiently. The scale of a program is not always under the control of an organization, as illustrated in the following example.

---

■■A new technology known as Magnetic-Miracle was shown to have a cost-effectiveness ratio of − $1000/QALY for treatment of arterial-venous malformations compared with the standard procedure at a major referral center. As a result of the enthusiasm produced by this report, 10 additional hospitals in the metropolitan area invested in Magnetic-Miracle equipment and expected to reproduce the results. To their surprise, the procedure was done infrequently in each hospital and the cost-effectiveness ratio for the metropolitan area as a whole was $100,000/QALY.     ■■

---

A cost-effectiveness analysis often makes the assumption that a procedure will be done frequently enough at any one particular site to efficiently use the personnel and equipment. This is presumably true in the site where the study is performed; however it cannot automatically be assumed to be true at future sites where the technology may be applied. Even accurate cost estimates made in one setting may need to be changed when extrapolated to another setting, as illustrated in the following example.

---

■■A cost-effectiveness analysis of a rehabilitative technique using physical therapy was estimated to be $40,000/QALY. You are very impressed with the procedure and believe it could be just as effective in Simplicity. However, you conclude that the cost per QALY is above the limit set in Simplicity. Upon closer

> examination you note that two-thirds of the costs resulted
> from the salary of the physical therapist, which on average are
> twice as high as in Simplicity.                              ▬

Extrapolation from one site to another is especially danger-
ous when the new site is quite different economically. These
factors need to be taken into account to the extent that the costs
of major inputs such as labor or equipment differ between the
setting of the study and the setting of the implementation. In this
example, the lower labor costs will reduce the cost per QALY
when the technique is used in Simplicity, and the procedure may
then be under the cost per QALY limit set in Simplicity.

Extrapolation between countries can be especially difficult
because of the many differences in costs and, at times, in effectiveness. When these adjustments are not made, we assume that
they would not alter the cost-effectiveness ratios. Thus, extrapolating costs from one setting to another requires us to look at
how the costs were calculated to be sure that the same conditions
apply at the new site.

Extrapolation assumptions are not limited to cost; they also
apply to effectiveness, as illustrated in the following examples
you encounter as Head of Health in Simplicity.

> ▬Intensive training of diabetics using a new device to fine tune
> blood sugar control was been demonstrated to cost $3,000/
> QALY when used on diabetics who had been self-administering
> insulin twice a day and monitoring their own blood sugar level.
> The authors concluded that widespread use of intensive training
> for all insulin-dependent diabetics with this new devise would
> be a very cost-effective measure.                           ▬

Before drawing this conclusion, it is important to realize
that the authors are assuming that the new device will be just as

effective when used on the larger group of all insulin-dependent diabetics. The study itself was done on the special group of severe diabetics who were already actively involved in monitoring their blood sugar levels. Success with a group of diabetic with less severe disease and a history of less active involvement in their care may not produce the same effectiveness. Thus effectiveness in one group does not necessarily imply effectiveness in another. Even when effectiveness appears to be the same in the short-run, longer-run effectiveness may be very different as illustrated in the following example.

---

■■A cost-effectiveness analysis of a vaccine that produced 10 years of protection from a disease called childrenspox was performed to examine the use of the vaccine on children with leukemia. The vaccine reduced the incidence of childrenspox with few side effect, none of which produced serious harm. The costs of hospitalization for children with leukemia was reduced. The cost-effectiveness analysis demonstrated that use of childrenspox vaccine in leukemic children actually reduced the cost while producing additional QALYs. The investigators were so impressed by the results that they advocated use of childrenspox vaccine for all children.           ■■

---

Think about what might happen if this conclusion were extrapolated to all children producing a recommendation to vaccinate all children. First, the benefits might be quite modest, because most healthy children will not have any difficulty handling childrenspox if they are infected as a child. However, the harms might be substantial especially if it was not possible to vaccinate every child, as would most likely be the case. If some children were missed, the general level of protection might keep them from being infected as children. However, they may experience childrenspox as adults when it may be a much more severe disease.

The cost savings from reduced hospitalization when the vaccine is given to healthy children will be much less than when the vaccine is given to children with leukemia. In addition, there will be increased costs of treating severely ill adults. Thus, the net costs may go up and the net benefit may go down if the vaccine is used on healthy children compared to its use on children with leukemia.

Thus far we have examined assumptions made in calculating the cost and calculating the effectiveness of treatment. As we discussed in chapter 5 there is another basic assumption built into cost-effectiveness analysis that often has implications regarding how the results are used. Cost-effectiveness analysis does not make any distinctions based on who receives the benefits and who receives the harms (i.e., it does not pay attention to the distribution of the outcomes).

The impact of this assumption can have important consequences with regard to how results of a cost-effectiveness analysis are used. Some of the effects of this assumption are illustrated in the following examples.

> As a result of the very low cost per QALY in a cost-effectiveness analysis, a rare element is being considered for inclusion in prenatal supplements offered to all pregnant women. The rare element has been shown to reduce the frequency of birth defects. This approach has been shown to be slightly more cost-effective than the alternative of supplementation of commonly consumed foods. The authors advocate the option to include the rare element in prenatal supplements rather than utilize food supplementation.

The cost-effectiveness analysis indicates that food supplementation costs slightly more per QALY. However, when looking at the options included in a cost-effectiveness analysis, it is important to realize that there are losers and gainers in many of the choices made. Cost-effectiveness looks at the size or magnitude of these gains and losses; it does not look at the types of people who receive the gains and the types of people who experience the losses.

It is very likely that poor women will receive less benefit from prenatal supplements than from food supplementation because they often receive less complete prenatal care. It may be argued that the poor deserve special attention to include them in the benefits of preventive interventions, especially when their inclusion does not reduce the benefits for others. Cost-effectiveness analysis pays no attention to the distribution of the benefits or the harms. Those who use these results, however, need to pay attention.

There are other types of distributional effects ignored by cost-effectiveness analysis as illustrated in the following example.

---

■A cost-effectiveness analysis compared the use of live Paralysis virus with killed Paralysis virus. Live Paralysis virus was more cost-effective because those who were vaccinated spread the virus—and thus its protection to those who were not vaccinated. Unfortunately, the live virus also causes a form of Paralysis in a very small percentage of vaccine recipients. The live virus can very rarely cause the vaccine-induced form of Paralysis among those who come in contact with the virus through exposure to a vaccinated person. In the study community the vaccination rate was 50%. The authors recommended that only live virus be used because they found much greater effectiveness at the same cost.                                  ■

---

The authors of this study assume that it is acceptable to cause a small number of cases of Paralysis among those who are exposed to individuals receiving the live vaccine. Cost-effectiveness analysis does not distinguish between voluntary and involuntary exposure to potential harm (or to potential benefit). In a community where only 50% of the children are vaccinated, this harm may be acceptable in exchange for the much larger benefits. However, there is another potential means of providing a high level of protection: increase the vaccination rate. In theory, if every child could be successfully vaccinated, there would be no need for the live virus, because its benefit of spreading protection to others would not be needed.

Thus, before accepting the results of a cost–effectiveness analysis it is important to recognize that the analysis does not take into account the distribution of the benefits or the harms. There may be times when the predictable distribution of the benefits and the harms makes a difference. At the very least, you need to ask yourself what type of people will receive the benefits and what type of people will receive the harms?

Cost-effectiveness analysis is performed at one point in time. It is like taking a snapshot, providing a static view of the world. After a treatment has been widely implemented dynamic changes can occur. The treatment may be used for new indications or at earlier or later times in the natural history of the disease. Changes in the way a procedure is used after it is implemented in a new setting may change its effectiveness and subsequently its costs as illustrated in the following example.

---

■■A cost-effectiveness analysis of a new procedure known as Pulverizer was performed to assess this procedure compared with surgical removal of kidney stones (the surgery-only option). Pulverizer was used whenever surgery was indicated followed by surgery if Pulverizer failed. The Pulverizer option was found to cost substantially less without any loss of effectiveness compared with the surgery-only option. The authors concluded that Pulverizer will reduce the costs of treating kidney stones and recommended that its use be extended to all patients with kidney stones.                                    ■

---

This type of extrapolation assumption occurs when we assume that the treatment option being studied will be used at the same point in the natural history of a disease when utilized in different settings. The authors' optimistic conclusions may not hold true. Traditionally, surgery for kidney stones occurs only after an extensive observation period, during which the stone is given every opportunity to pass on its own. The widespread availability of Pulverizer and greater patient acceptance may mean that Pulverizer is used soon after the diagnosis of kidney stones. Thus, even if Pulverizer is more cost-effective per use than surgery, it may increase costs substantially without substantially increasing the benefit, especially if it is performed on large numbers of patients whose stones would have previously been allowed to pass on their own.

At times, the introduction of new treatments can alter the natural history of a disease in unexpected ways that can alter the costs and effectiveness of therapy, as illustrated in the following example.

---

■■The cost-effectiveness ratio of Pulverizer in the previous study was 80% of the cost per QALY compared with surgery. After adopting Pulverizer only as a substitute for surgery in your hospital, you read that on average kidney stones return after 8 years with surgery and after 4 years with Pulverizer. You wonder how this might alter the cost-effectiveness ratio.    ■■■

---

In the short run, this increase in recurrences would have little effect on costs. However, after the recurrences began to occur, costs would increase and eventually there would be twice as many uses of Pulverizer and an increased cost compared with the estimates made in the original cost-effectiveness analysis. Thus, it is important to explicitly recognize the assumptions made so we can look for new evidence and quickly pull back if new evidence suggests that the assumptions were not accurate.

At times, it is critical to incorporate any dynamic changes that are predicable at the time the cost-effectiveness analysis is conducted or else the results may lead to very misleading conclusions, as illustrated in the following example.

■As a result of the SADS epidemic, an old disease called Trouble Breathing (TB) has again begun to spread. There is concern that an epidemic is about to emerge. An intensive treatment program is available that has been shown to be effective in controlling the spread from the small number of cases of TB that have occurred in Simplicity. A cost-effectiveness analysis looking at the high costs of this treatment relative to the benefits for those with TB and their likely contacts concluded that the treatment had a very high cost per QALY and therefore was not cost-effective.                                     ■

Before accepting this conclusion, it is important to recognize that this analysis has assumed that TB can be just as effectively controlled at a later time. However, once an epidemic emerges it may be very difficult to control. In addition, once an infectious disease has begun to spread there may be considerable social disruption and financial costs, as people go to great lengths to avoid those they believe may jeopardize their health.

Thus, some diseases and some treatments deserve priority above and beyond their immediate impact on effectiveness or costs. Infectious diseases such as TB need to be brought under control because they jeopardize the health of others and make economic and social activity less secure and predictable. Short-term calculations of cost-effectiveness can hide much larger long-term costs and secondary effects that occur because of fear of disease.

Whenever the longer term impact of an intervention can be anticipated, it is possible to incorporate these changes into a cost-effectiveness analysis. When these effects are not included, the results of a cost-effectiveness analysis may be misleading.

In addition to the preceding assumptions, you realize after reading the cost-effectiveness literature that sometimes by the time the study is completed and published the technology that was being evaluated is already technologically out-of-date. The pace of technological change may be so rapid in many fields that cost-effectiveness analyses may be out-of-date by the time they are published because the costs are rapidly changing, sometimes decreasing as more experience is gained in applying the new technology. Alternatively, the technology examined in the cost-effectiveness analysis may have already been replaced by a new approach.

■■Having learned the uses and potential misuses of cost-effectiveness analysis, you are able to function very well as the Head of Health for Simplicity. As a result of your cost-effective decisions, Simplicity achieves a very high standard of health.

A cost-effective approach to using Pneumogone and treating Glandular Overactivity has been successfully implemented. Both Paralysis and Coronary have been largely prevented using the resources saved through your wise decisions. The indications for Cardiomagic are now carefully defined so it rarely needs to be paid for out of pocket.

The SADS epidemic has not been conquered but your persistent efforts to implement new cost-effective measures have reduced the rate of new disease and extended the life-expectancy and quality of life of those in whom SADS develops. Prenatal care and routine infant and pediatric care have prevented or cured most diseases of children and adolescents, or rehabilitated those who experienced them. Emergency care, adult curative care, and prevention of chronic disease has delayed death among adults. Very few of Simplicity's citizens die before retirement age.

After retirement, continued preventive, curative, and rehabilitative services keep the citizens of Simplicity in good health for an average of 15 years. Most citizens of Simplicity die at home after experiencing a brief illness either soon before or soon after their 80th birthday.

Despite your successes in improving the health of Simplicity, some of your citizens unfavorably compare Simplicity to the similar neighboring community of High-Tech. Compared to High-Tech they claim that the health system of Simplicity has two basic limitations: (1) Infants continue to die during the first month of life because little is done for those with severe disabilities, and (2) in Simplicity, after age 80, the goals of health care are to provide comfort and to increase function, but not to extend life.

In High-Tech everyone with an illness gets the best care

possible. All infants receive the newest technological advances to extend their lives as long as possible. In High-Tech, as opposed to Simplicity, the elderly receive intensive medical care, regardless of age. Unless the patient insists, the citizens of High-Tech are required to die in a hospital after receiving the maximum care possible.

In High-Tech they have reduced the death rate among those under one year of age by saving most premature infants. In addition, they have extended the life span for those citizens who in Simplicity usually die in their early 80s.

## WHAT ELSE DO YOU WANT TO KNOW ABOUT HIGH-TECH? WOULD YOU PREFER TO LIVE IN HIGH-TECH?

After some questioning you discover that in High-Tech, efforts to prevent disease sometimes take a back seat to efforts to cure disease. For instance, in High-Tech, the SADS epidemic has continued, resulting in an increased number of cases of SADS; this has occurred at the same time that there have been major advances in treating the disease, once present.

You also investigate how much High-Tech is spending relative to their resources. The percentage of gross domestic product spent on health is a useful first approximation. Simplicity spends less than 10%; High-Tech spends almost 15%, or 1.5 times as much per person as Simplicity.

You now realize that the new system in Simplicity has worked reasonably well. It has improved the health of the citizens of Simplicity while controlling costs. You recognize that there are no limits to how much can be spent on health care. Perhaps spending more can produce additional benefits. But there have to be limits; setting those limits is never easy. Making decisions about health care is not simple, even in Simplicity.

# SUGGESTED READINGS

## PART I: BENEFITS AND HARMS

Sox HC, Blatt MA, Higgins MC, Marton KI. Medical decision making. Boston: Butterworth, 1988.

Weinstein MC, Fineberg HV. Clinical decision analysis. Philiadelphia: WB Saunders, 1980.

Baron J. Thinking and deciding. New York: Cambridge University Press, 1988.

Dawes RM. Rational choice in an uncertain world. San Diego: Harcourt, Brace, Jovanovich, 1988.

Yates JF, ed. Risk-taking behavior. New York: John Wiley and Sons, 1992.

## PART II: BENEFITS, HARMS, AND COSTS

Kamlet MS. The comparative benefits modeling project—a framework for cost-utility analysis of government health care programs. U.S. Department of Health and Human Services Public Health Service. U.S. Government Printing Office, Washington, D.C. 1992.

Warner KE, Luce BR. Cost-benefit and cost-effectiveness analysis in health care. Ann Arbor: Health Administration Press, 1982.

Drummond MF, Stoddert GL, Torrence GW. Methods for the economic evaluation of health care programmes. Oxford Medical Publications, 1987.

Detsky AS, Naglie GA. A clinician's guide to cost-effectiveness analysis. Ann Intern Med 1990;113:147–154.

# APPENDIX
## Summary of Steps and Assumptions in Harm-Benefit and Cost-Effectiveness Analysis

### HARM-BENEFIT ANALYSIS

Harm-benefit analysis, often performed using decision trees and called decision analysis, is based on expected utility theory. Expected utility asks "how do we maximize the net benefit to the average patient while ignoring the budget constraints?" Effectiveness is calculated as an overall expected utility and is often expressed in units known as quality-adjusted lives. It is possible to convert quality-adjusted lives to quality-adjusted life-years if the average life-expectancy is known. Whenever an overall expected utility is calculated it is possible to convert this number to an adjusted number-needed-to-treat.

The following summarizes the steps that take place in the performance of a harm-benefit decision analysis using expected utility theory.

### Steps in Harm-Benefit Analysis Using Expected Utility Theory

1. Identify all potential treatment alternatives relevant to accomplishing your goal. Determine which of these alternatives should receive active consideration.
2. Draw a decision tree that identifies, for each alternative receiving active consideration, the decision points and the chance points, chronologically, and includes them as decision nodes (*squares*) and chance nodes (*circles*) in the decision tree.
3. Identify all potential outcomes of each treatment alternative, placing these potential outcomes at the right-hand terminal branches of the decision tree.
4. Prune back the decision tree eliminating all except the important outcomes.
5. Estimate the probabilities that follow each chance node.
6. Calculate the path probabilities for each potential outcome of the decision tree by multiplying together the successive probabilities (folding back the decision tree).
7. Obtain utilities for each potential outcome of each of the treatment options included in the decision tree.
8. Calculate expected utilities for each potential outcome of each treat-

ment alternative by multiplying the path probability times the utility of each potential outcome.

9. Calculate the overall expected utility for each of the treatment options by adding the expected utilities from each of the potential outcomes of a particular treatment option (average out the decision tree).

10. Compare the expected utilities of two or more options by directly comparing their overall expected utilities or by calculating an adjusted number-needed-to-treat.

11. Perform a sensitivity analysis to determine the extent to which the results are altered by using alternative numerical values for one or more probability or utility.

### Assumptions of Harm–Benefit Analysis

1. The options relevant to accomplishing your goal have all been considered.

#### Assumptions related to probabilities

2. The decision tree for each option includes all the important probabilities that affect the decision to choose that option.

3. The probabilities derived from a past period of time accurately reflect the probabilities in the future.

4. The outcome states are permanent and cannot recur. If this is not the case, mathematical models, which incorporate transition states known as Markov processes, should be used.

5. The mutually exclusive assumption: an individual will experience only one of the potential outcomes.

6. Equal proportion benefit in a new setting: when using probabilities of benefit derived from other settings, it is assumed that the benefit will be a constant proportion of those receiving the treatment.

7. Equal difference of harm in a new setting: when using probabilities of harm derived from other settings it is assumed that the difference in probability of harm between treatment groups will be the same.

8. The independence assumption: the probability of occurrence of one event does not influence the probability of occurrence of other event(s).

#### Assumptions related to utilities and timing

9. Death is the worst possible outcome: there are no utilities worse than death.

10. It-does-not-matter-how-you-get-there assumption: death or other

outcomes have the same utility regardless of the route a patient takes in getting there.

11. Personal impact assumption: utilities are judged by the impact they have on the decision-maker or the individual immediately affected rather than from a social perspective.

12. Stability of utilities assumption: estimates of utilities prior to experiencing an event will not change after the event has been experienced.

13. Utility units are all equal: a unit difference is valued the same regardless of where it is on the scale, even including a unit that means the difference between being alive and being dead.

14. Discounting for harms and for benefits is performed if all events do not occur in the immediate future.

### Assumptions related to deviations from expected utility

15. Attitudes do not matter: attitudes toward guarantees, gambles, regret, and responsibilities do not influence the decision or balance each other out.

16. The manner of presentation is not important: optimism versus pessimism, ambiguity, and issues of control do not influence decision-making or balance each other out.

### Assumptions related to choice of decision-making principles

17. Action inclinations are not important: the action inclination of the decision-maker does not influence the choice of treatment options.

18. Maximize expected utility is the governing decision principle: alternative principles, such as maximizing full benefit, satisficing, and minimizing harm are not being used as the governing decision principle.

In addition to these specific assumptions, we also assume that the probabilities and utilities which are being used were accurately obtained and that the utility score is independent of the probability.

## COST-EFFECTIVENESS ANALYSIS

Cost-effectiveness analysis is designed to maximize the benefits to society, that is to all individuals in society including those who are immediately affected by the benefits and harms as well as those who are not immediately affected by the benefits and harms. Specifically, it is designed to maximize the overall effectiveness received by the individuals in the society when there are budget constraints or a limit or cap on how much can be spent.

There is often an inherent conflict between treatments which provide the greatest net benefit to an individual and treatments which provide the greatest net benefit to a society.

Cost-effectiveness analysis, specifically the version of cost-effectiveness analysis called cost-utility analysis, is a method used to compare the monetary cost per unit of effectiveness as measured in quality-adjusted-life-years (QALYs). It is designed to allow comparison of potential treatment options designed to improve or maintain health.

In contrast to cost-benefit analysis, cost-effectiveness analysis does not place a monetary value on a QALY and it does not allow us to compare health intervention with other possible uses of money.

### Steps in a Cost-Effectiveness Analysis

1. Identify all potential treatment options relevant to accomplishing your goal. Determine which of these alternatives should receive active consideration.
2. Calculate the benefits minus the harms or the effectiveness of each relevant option or obtain it from a harm-benefit analysis (done from a social perspective).
3. Adjust effectiveness measured in quality-adjusted lives to take into account life-expectancy and thereby calculate quality-adjusted-life-years (QALYs) as the units of effectiveness.
4. Calculate the costs of treatment including medical input costs (sometimes called direct costs) and nonmedical input costs (sometimes called indirect costs).
5. Discount the cost, benefits, and harms using the same discount rate.
6. Calculate the cost-effectiveness ratio.
7. Calculate an incremental cost-effectiveness ratio to compare treatment options whenever the options may produce different numbers of QALYs and have different costs.
8. Determine in which of the four cost-QALY quadrants the results are located to correctly interpret the meaning of a positive or of a negative sign. If the treatment options lie in the right lower quadrant (greater effectiveness and less cost), declare the treatment option cost-effective.
9. If an option lies in the left upper quadrant (greater cost for greater effectiveness) decide if the increased effectiveness is worth the increased cost.
10. If an option lies in the right lower quadrant (less effectiveness for less cost) decide if the reduced cost is worth the reduced effectiveness.

## Assumptions of cost-effectiveness analysis

Cost-effectiveness analysis uses the results of harm-benefit analysis in the denominator of the cost-effectiveness ratios. However, the harms and benefits should be calculated from a social perspective. Thus, it makes all the assumptions required to perform a harm-benefit analysis. In addition, it assumes that effectiveness is measured in quality-adjusted-life-years (QALYs) that accurately estimate the life-expectancy of the average person who receives the benefit and the average person who experiences the harm. In addition, a cost-effectiveness analysis may make the following assumptions.

## Assumptions in calculating effectiveness and costs in addition to those required for harm-benefit decision analysis

1. Estimates of utility are constant regardless of the length of remaining life.
2. The life-expectancy accurately reflects the probabilities of death of those who are being considered for treatment.
3. Costs reflect opportunity costs (i.e., the value of alternatives that could be achieved with the same resources).
4. The costs (as well as benefits and harms) are included from the social perspective, that is, they include all impact costs of the intervention regardless of who pays, but they do not include the medical or nonmedical costs of success.
5. Costs, benefits, and harms have all been discounted at the same discount rate.

## Assumptions related to acceptance of the results of a cost-effectiveness analysis

6. Institutional settings in which the results of a cost-effectiveness analysis are being considered for implementation will experience the same costs and benefits as society as a whole. Thus, factors such as fixed costs, partial payments, and reimbursements that do not match resource use will not influence the acceptance of the results.
7. Extrapolation of the results to a new setting will not be altered by effectiveness or cost considerations, such as economies or diseconomies of scale or different cost structures for resources in different societies.
8. Distributional considerations that take into account the types of individuals who will be losers and those who will be gainers does not influence acceptance of the results.
9. Dynamic changes expected after implementation, such as widespread use beyond initial indications, resistance to the treatment effect, and epidemic potentials, do not influence acceptance of the results.

# INDEX